A Review of Selected International Aircraft Spares Pooling Programs

Lessons Learned for F-35 Spares Pooling

Mark A. Lorell, James Pita

RAND Project AIR FORCE

Prepared for the United States Air Force
Approved for public release; distribution unlimited

For more information on this publication, visit www.rand.org/t/RR999

Library of Congress Cataloging-in-Publication Data is available for this publication.

ISBN: 978-0-8330-9028-7

Preface

The F-35 Joint Strike Fighter (JSF) program includes development and procurement of three different variants for the U.S. Air Force (USAF), U.S. Navy (USN), and U.S. Marine Corps (USMC). In addition, the F-35 program has a major international component. Eight foreign participant nations (Australia, Canada, Denmark, Italy, the Netherlands, Norway, Turkey, and the United Kingdom) shared in the system's development and procurement.[1] In September 2012, the United States and the foreign participant nations agreed that F-35 sustainment assets (spare propulsion systems, support equipment, and all JSF air system spares) would be managed as a single global pool, which would be centrally managed by the F-35 product support manager. However, in the formal agreement establishing this pool, language was included that allows participants to opt out, should a nation desire to establish (and be willing to pay for) a separate stock of assets not subject to shared management.

A separate RAND Project AIR FORCE (PAF) draft report (not available to the general public) examines potential savings and risks associated with USAF participation in the F-35 global spares pool:

> Ronald G. McGarvey, Edward G. Keating, Mark A. Lorell, James Pita, John G. Drew, Daniel M. Romano, Joseph V. Vesely, and Robert A. Guffey, *United States Air Force Participation in the F-35 Global Spares Pool: Advantages and Risks*, unpublished RAND Corporation research, 2015.

This companion report supports the major research objectives examined in the principal report by reviewing other selected historical and current international military aircraft spares pooling programs involving the United States, major European North Atlantic Treaty Organization (NATO) allies, and other U.S. allies. The purpose of this part of the analysis is to glean lessons from other historical or current military aircraft programs in which spares pooling was attempted or implemented.

This research was conducted within the Resource Management Program of PAF for the project "Identifying and Mitigating Risks to USAF Eventuating from the F-35 Global Asset Pool," sponsored by Maj Gen John Cooper, then Director of Logistics, Office of the Deputy Chief of Staff for Logistics, Installations and Mission Support, Headquarters USAF (AF/A4L).

This report should be of interest to logisticians, operators, and acquisition professionals throughout the USAF and the Department of Defense.

---

[1] In addition, there are currently two Foreign Military Sales (FMS) participants, Israel and Japan.

RAND Project AIR FORCE

RAND Project AIR FORCE (PAF), a division of the RAND Corporation, is the U.S. Air Force's federally funded research and development center for studies and analyses. PAF provides the Air Force with independent analyses of policy alternatives affecting the development, employment, combat readiness, and support of current and future air, space, and cyber forces. Research is conducted in four programs: Force Modernization and Employment; Manpower, Personnel, and Training; Resource Management; and Strategy and Doctrine. The research reported here was prepared under contract FA7014-06-C-0001.

Additional information about PAF is available on our website:
http://www.rand.org/paf/

Table of Contents

Summary

Introduction and Research Approach

The F-35 Joint Strike Fighter (JSF) is a fifth-generation stealth fighter whose system development was shared by nine countries: the United States (for which the F-35 is being jointly procured by the U.S. Air Force [USAF], U.S. Navy [USN], and U.S. Marine Corps [USMC]), Australia, Canada, Denmark, Italy, the Netherlands, Norway, Turkey, and the United Kingdom. In 2012, these countries agreed that F-35 sustainment assets (spare propulsion systems, support equipment, and all air system spares) would be managed as a single global pool, which would be centrally managed by the F-35 production support manager. Since then, participating countries and the Joint Program Office (JPO) have developed a series of decision memoranda and draft business rules to govern such matters as the allocation of scarce parts, what happens when a partner cannot fully fund its share of program costs, and how the program will manage divergence from a common configuration baseline. In the formal agreement establishing this pool, language was also included to allow participants to opt out of the global pool, should a nation desire to establish (and be willing to pay for) a separate stock of assets.

A separate RAND Project AIR FORCE (PAF) principal report (unavailable to the general public) provides an assessment of potential savings and risks associated with USAF participation in the F-35 global spares pool.[2] Savings arise from the need to stock fewer total spare parts than if all the participants operated on a purely national basis because of differentials in demand, particularly for high-cost parts with a low failure rate.[3] However, there are also risks involved in pooling spare parts. RAND research identified three main risk areas for U.S. participation in a proposed F-35 international spares pool:

- ensuring security of supply and prioritizing the allocation of scarce spares resources
- configuration management and control, and managing technology innovators versus laggards
- managing "shirkers," or those participants unable or unwilling to pay their agreed share to the spares pooling effort.

This companion report reviews other selected historical and current international military aircraft spares pooling programs involving the United States, European North Atlantic Treaty

---

[2] Ronald G. McGarvey, Edward G. Keating, Mark A. Lorell, James Pita, John G. Drew, Daniel M. Romano, Joseph V. Vesely, and Robert A. Guffey, *United States Air Force Participation in the F-35 Global Spares Pool: Advantages and Risks*, unpublished RAND Corporation research, 2015.

[3] McGarvey et al., 2015, p. xii.

Organization (NATO) allies, and other U.S. allies. The purpose of this analysis is twofold: We attempt to discover whether these three risk areas were important issues of concern among the participants and, if so, how these concerns were mitigated or resolved. It was hoped that such analysis might provide important historical lessons learned that could inform the final structuring the F-35 spares pooling initiative.

We systematically reviewed a major selection of past attempts at global spares pooling in order to gain insights and lessons that might be applicable to USAF participation in F-35 global spares pooling. Initially, the focus was on programs with international spares sharing among foreign allies involving fighter/attack aircraft with or without U.S. participation. Because there were so few examples of pooling for fighter/attack aircraft and very little information available, we later expanded our search to include other types of military aircraft. Nearly all the examples we examined involved European allies.[4]

The first part of this document reviews the historical programs RAND examined, discusses the principal reasons so few successful programs resulted from these efforts, and shares how these reasons may inform plans for F-35 global spares pooling. The second part of the document focuses in much greater detail on the C-17 Globemaster III Sustainment Partnership and later C-17 Global Integrated Sustainment Partnership (GISP), one of the few successful past global spares programs implemented, in order to assess its relevance to the F-35 program.

Detailed Research Findings on Historical International Spares Pooling Initiatives

Historically NATO Has Strongly Encouraged Spares Pooling, But Until Recently Examples of Successful Spares Pooling Have Been Rare, Especially in Fighter Programs

Most major European military aircraft programs during the 1960s through 2000 involved collaborative development and procurement, yet few of these programs resulted in successful comprehensive spares pooling. Most of the historic programs prior to Eurofighter that have succeeded could be described as exhibiting one or more of the following characteristics: One partner plays a dominant role, such as the United States in the F-104G program; there is full

---

[4] There were important limitations on the quality and quantity of information we were able to collect. This task of the overall research effort was limited both in time and resources. As a result, we were largely limited to using open source information. For older programs from the 1960s through the 1980s, we were unable to find credible data and information on various programs and some of their characteristics. We also occasionally encountered significant challenges in obtaining comprehensive open source information on recent foreign programs, due to foreign government and contractor sensitivities. This was particularly true in the case of the Eurofighter Typhoon program after the restructuring of the pooled spares contracts in 2012. Nonetheless, we believe we were able to collect sufficient information to support the analysis presented here.

international ownership and operation of the entire weapon system (such as the NATO Airborne Warning and Control System [AWACS] program); there are ad hoc bilateral relationships between small partners; or there are temporary sharing agreements, such as combined deployments and exercises, by the F-16 European Participating Air Force (EPAF) nations.

Based on the historical examples we have examined from the F-106G in the 1960s through the current Eurofighter Typhoon and EH90 helicopter programs, we determined that the first two challenges (security and resource allocation and configuration management and control) were among the most important barriers inhibiting the adoption of effective spares pooling in past historical programs. For a variety of reasons, the third challenge (managing shirkers) did not seem to play as significant a role in past historical programs.

A Complicated International Spares Pooling Scheme Was Adopted in the Four-Nation Eurofighter Program in the Early 2000s, But Results Were Mixed and Serious Spares Shortages Arose During Combat Deployments

In the mid-1980s, Germany, Italy, Spain, and the United Kingdom launched the Eurofighter Typhoon program, the largest and most ambitious fighter development and procurement program in European history. In 1997, the partner nations signed an integrated logistics agreement memorandum of understanding. Four years later, in 2001, the Eurofighter partners established the Eurofighter Industrial Exchange and Repair Service (IERS), which aimed to implement comprehensive international spares pooling by 2005. However, the contentious, complex, and politically driven work-sharing arrangements on the program undermined the implementation of an economically optimal spares pooling strategy and resulted in the negotiation of 11 separate support contracts for the IERS.

According to extensive investigative studies conducted by the United Kingdom (UK) National Audit Office (NAO) and by the House of Commons Committee of Public Accounts, whose findings were published in 2011, the international spares pooling contracts did not work well. According to these studies, the international spares pooling contracts led to significant shortages of spares for the Royal Air Force (RAF) Typhoons, negatively affecting readiness and availability rates.[5] Some press reports claimed that these spares shortages had led to a reduction in Typhoon readiness and availability rates during combat operations in Libya after RAF Typhoons had deployed to forward operating bases in Italy.[6]

---

[5] Comptroller and Auditor General, United Kingdom National Audit Office, *Ministry of Defence: Management of the Typhoon Project,* HC 755 Session 2010–2011, London, HMSO, March 2, 2011; and United Kingdom House of Commons, Committee of Public Accounts, *Management of the Typhoon Project*, Thirteenth Report of Session 2010–2012, London, HMSO, April 15, 2011.

[6] For example, see BBC News, "RAF Typhoon Jets Grounded Owing to Spares Shortages," April 15, 2011; Ian Drury, "RAF Strips Jets for Spare Parts: Typhoons Torn Up for Libya Air Fleet," *Daily Mail,* June 16, 2011; and Marco Giannangeli, "RAF Hit By Crisis Over Spares for Fighter Jets: Nearly Half the RAF's New Typhoon Jets Are Grounded Because of Maintenance and Lack of Spare Parts," *The Daily Express*, December 4, 2011.

The Eurofighter partners finally restructured and simplified the support arrangements for Eurofighter in 2012 when the existing 11 support contracts were consolidated down to four contracts. A major portion of these contracts involved direct relationships between each nation's air force and its own national industry. We do not have adequate information to assess the extent to which this restructuring includes true spares pooling.

There Are Current Examples of Successful Spares Pooling, But They Differ from the Proposed F-35 Pool in Important Ways

There have been a few successful spares pooling programs in the past, but they differ from the proposed F-35 pool in important ways. The only sustained successes to date appear to be programs in which the foreign international partners had very little stake in the design and development stages; the United States subsidized the program; and the USAF exercised clear technological, financial, and economic leverage. In the case of fighter aircraft, there are no examples of successful programs—with the possible exception of the F-104G in the early 1960s, which took place in an industrial environment much different than today, and perhaps the recently restructured Eurofighter support program, for which we lack information and data.

The most successful case of spares pooling for which we were able to acquire extensive information is the C-17 GISP program. In the case of the C-17 GISP, the foreign partners do not have major design and industrial stakes in the development and production of the aircraft; moreover, their fleets are relatively small. Thus, the USAF is able to maintain common configuration by requiring all partners to make all of the upgrades and modifications that the USAF makes. In case of parts shortages, the USAF's Air Mobility Command exercises the authority to allocate scarce resources. Shirking (failure of a participant to fully fund its share of the program) has not been a problem because the foreign partner fleets are small.

In contrast, the F-35 partner nations have major design and industrial stakes in the development and production of the aircraft, and the disparity in fleet size is much lower than for the C-17. Thus, it is not surprising that under the draft business rules for F-35 spares sharing, no U.S. service has primacy over allocation decisions for scarce spares and no U.S. service dictates configuration management. Therefore, any F-35 spares pooling initiative is likely to entail the kinds of risks and challenges encountered on previous collaborative fighter efforts, such as Tornado or Eurofighter, which to date have not, in general, led to satisfactory spares pooling programs.

Overall Summary Research Findings on Historical International Spares Pooling Initiatives

Based on this analysis, we arrived at the following lessons learned from historical international spares pooling initiatives, which are relevant to the current F-35 international spares pooling initiative:

- The negotiation of international spares pooling programs for common major weapon systems has been attempted many times since the 1960s, but they have proven to be very difficult to implement. There are far more failures than successes.
- We found three major historical barriers to the successful negotiation of spares pooling programs in the past. The first two were similar to the first two risk areas identified in the principal RAND report: (1) security of supply and prioritization of scarce spares assets and (2) configuration management and management of innovators versus laggards. These two challenges can be difficult to overcome unless one partner plays a dominant role in the pooling arrangements.
- Shirking did not seem to be a critical problem on past programs.
- A major historical challenge, especially for all-European programs or programs in which all the partners were roughly of equivalent size and influence, was conflicting industrial, technological, and economic interests and objectives.
- The most successful historical programs were characterized by a single dominant partner that could establish the ground rules and resource allocation priorities, as well as control configuration. At the same time, successful programs made major efforts to ensure fairness, equality, and transparency for all partners, based on relative contribution and need.
- Several recent programs, including the C-17 GISP program in particular, provide insights into specific policy measures that, based on program experience, facilitate a more successful program structure for spares pooling involving the USAF. These policy measures include the following issues and factors:

    o U.S. export control laws and regulations can be a significant barrier to successful spares pooling. The most successful past programs have mitigated this problem by retaining U.S. ownership of all spares except when they are installed in ally-owned aircraft. In the case of the C-17 GISP program, Boeing, as the single point exporter, controls and allocates parts until they are installed on allied aircraft.
    o Two critical keys to the success of configuration control and encouragement of innovation on the C-17 GISP program are (1) the requirement that all aircraft in the pool conform to U.S. configuration standards, with the proviso that (2) the U.S. Air Force pays for the nonrecurring costs of upgrading the aircraft.
    o Contract incentives for the prime contractor to meet international fleetwide performance metrics and priorities require a splitting out of the smaller foreign fleets with separately calculated metrics so that these fleets are serviced with the same priority as the larger U.S. fleet.
    o The above factors may only work well on a program in which the U.S. fleet is significantly larger than all foreign fleets and in which the U.S. Air Force is clearly the dominant customer, as in the case of the C-17 GISP program. This situation may not hold equally well for the F-35 program, particularly for variants such as the F-35B in which U.S. dominance may not be nearly as clear-cut.

Acknowledgments

Many people inside and outside of the Air Force provided valuable assistance and support to our work.[7] We thank Maj Gen John Cooper, Director of Logistics, Office of the Deputy Chief of Staff for Logistics, Installations and Mission Support, Headquarters USAF (AF/A4L), for sponsoring this project. On the AF/A4L staff, we thank Col Kyle Matyi, Lt Col David Seitz, Guy Fowl, and John Gunselman for providing us with access to subject matter experts both within the USAF and within the JPO and for sharing their feedback during interim project update briefings. At the JPO, we thank GP CAPT (UK) Peter Grinsted and his staff, in particular CAPT (USN) Leigh Ackart and Enass Saad-Pappas, for providing us with the background materials and data necessary to conduct this analysis. At Headquarters Air Force Materiel Command, we thank Bob McCormick for sharing his supply chain subject matter expertise and assisting us with many data searches. Col Mark H. Mol at Hill Air Force Base (AFB) and Col David Morgan at Robins AFB helped us in learning about historical precedents. LtCol Cor van der Gaag of the Royal Netherlands Air Force and Hannes Ross, former director of advanced programs at the European Aeronautic Defence and Space Company Munich, assisted our inquiries into analogous European programs.

At RAND, we thank our colleagues Laura Baldwin, Sean Bednarz, Marygail Brauner, John Halliday, Michael Kennedy, and Robert Tripp for sharing their insights and suggestions during the development of our final project briefing and this draft report. We thank Megan McKeever for her assistance in the preparation of this document.

We are particularly grateful for the constructive criticism and suggestions provided by the formal RAND reviewers of this document, Edward Keating and Grover Dunn. In addition, Lara Schmidt, associate director of PAF, made substantial substantive inputs for this document in her capacity as overseer of PAF quality assurance. The inputs from these RAND colleagues measurably improved the quality of this document.

That we received help and insights from those acknowledged above should not be taken to imply that they concur with the findings presented in this report. As always, the analysis and conclusions are solely the responsibility of the authors.

---

[7] All office symbols and military ranks are listed as of the time of this research.

Abbreviations

ADV	Air Defence Variant
AF/A4L	Director of Logistics, Office of the Deputy Chief of Staff for Logistics, Installations and Mission Support, Headquarters USAF
AFB	Air Force Base
AMC	Air Mobility Command
AMP	Airlift Management Program
ASP	Afloat Spares Package
AWACS	Airborne Warning and Control System
BSP	Base Spares Package
CLS	Contractor Logistics Support
CPO	Combined Program Office
CTOL	conventional takeoff and landing
CV	Carrier-Based Version
DoD	Department of Defense
DSP	Deployment Spares Package
EADS	European Aeronautic Defence and Space Company
ECM	electronic countermeasures
EDA	European Defense Agency
EPAF	European Participating Air Forces
EU	European Union
FAD	Force Activity Designator
FLIR	forward-looking infrared
FMS	Foreign Military Sales
FPAA	Fleet Performance Aircraft Availability
GDIT	General Dynamics Information Technology
GISP	Global Integrated Sustainment Partnership
GSP	Global Spares Package
HAW	Heavy Airlift Wing

IDS	interdictor/strike
IERS	Industrial Exchange and Repair Service
ITC	Integrated Training Center
IWSSC	International Weapon System Support Centre
JESB	Joint Executive Steering Board
JPO	Joint Program Office
JSF	Joint Strike Fighter
LDHD	low-density high-demand
MAP	Military Assistance Program
MELS	Mutual Emergency Logistics Support
MICAP	Mission Impaired Capability Awaiting Parts
MILCON	military construction
MLU	midlife update
MoU	memorandum of understanding
MRCA	Multi-Role Combat Aircraft
MRTT	Multirole Tanker Transport
MSIP	Multinational Stage Improvement Program
NAEW&C	NATO Airborne Early Warning and Control Program
NAHEMA	NATO Helicopter Management Agency
NAMMA	NATO Airlift Multirole-Combat Management Agency
NAMSO	NATO Maintenance and Supply Organization
NAO	National Audit Office
NATO	North Atlantic Treaty Organization
NETMA	NATO Eurofighter and Tornado Management Agency
NMC	not mission-capable
NSPA	NATO Support and Procurement Agency
O&S	Operating and Support
OEM	original equipment manufacturer
P&S	Pooling and Sharing
PAF	RAND Project AIR FORCE
PBL	Performance-Based Logistics

RAF	Royal Air Force
RDT&E	Research, Development, Test, and Evaluation
SAC	Strategic Airlift Capability
SAC/HAW	Strategic Airlift Capability/Heavy Airlift Wing
SAR	Selected Acquisition Report
SEPECAT	*Société Européenne de Production de l'Avion Ecole de Combat et d'Appui Tactique* (European Production Company for the Combat Trainer and Tactical Attack Aircraft)
STOVL	short takeoff and vertical landing
TNMCS	total not-mission-capable for supply
UK	United Kingdom
USAF	U.S. Air Force
USMC	U.S. Marine Corps
USN	U.S. Navy
VF	virtual fleet
WEU	Western European Union

1. Introduction and Overview

The F-35 Joint Strike Fighter (JSF) is a fifth-generation stealth fighter whose system development was shared by nine countries: the United States (for which the F-35 is being jointly procured by the U.S. Air Force [USAF], U.S. Navy [USN], and U.S. Marine Corps [USMC]), Australia, Canada, Denmark, Italy, the Netherlands, Norway, Turkey, and the United Kingdom. In 2012, these countries agreed that F-35 sustainment assets (spare propulsion systems, support equipment, and all air system spares) would be managed as a single global pool, which would be centrally managed by the F-35 production support manager. Since then, participating countries and the Joint Program Office (JPO) have developed a series of decision memoranda and draft business rules to govern such matters as the allocation of scarce parts, what happens when a partner cannot fully fund its share of program costs, and how the program will manage divergence from a common configuration baseline. In the formal agreement establishing this pool, language was also included to allow participants to opt out of the global pool, should a nation desire to establish (and be willing to pay for) a separate stock of assets.

RAND Project AIR FORCE (PAF) recently examined potential savings and risks associated with USAF participation in the F-35 global spares pool. The findings from this research are reported in a recent document (not available to the general public) entitled *United States Air Force Participation in the F-35 Global Spares Pool: Advantages and Risks*.[8]

This report is a supplemental companion document to the principal research document identified above. The principal document presents the main RAND analysis of the F-35 spares pooling proposal and a discussion of the theoretical benefits and likely risks to the Air Force of joining such a proposed pooling initiative, based on the RAND analysis of the proposed business rules for the pooling initiative. It also presents a summary of the material presented in this companion document covering other historical cases of spares pooling.

The principal document examined the theoretical benefits of spares pooling, which are mainly related to cost. This report identified three major mechanisms for cost savings from spares pooling:

- The *integer phenomenon*, in which there is an expensive part that rarely fails. With a number of air forces each possessing a relatively small fleet of aircraft, without pooling, each of these air forces would have to retain some of these high-cost parts, no matter how small its fleet was. With pooling, a smaller number of these parts would need to be stocked because they could be shared among all the air forces safely due to the high reliability of the part.
- *Reduced variability* from pooling particularly favors smaller air forces because a

---

[8] McGarvey et al., 2015.

larger pool reduces relative lead time variability in relation to total demand.

- *Offsetting demand* refers to each partner needing a specific part at different times, leading to some but not complete overlap of demand for the same part. This permits a pool to stock a smaller total number of parts than would be the case if all the air forces stocked separately just for themselves.[9]

However, the RAND analysis suggests that spares pooling also poses some risks. The principal document used different quantitative, economic, theoretical, and other methodologies to arrive at the conclusion that the business rules proposed for the F-35 spares pooling initiatives posed three main risks for the Air Force. These three main risks involve the following:

- prioritizing the allocation of scarce pooled resources and ensuring security of supply
- managing technology innovators versus laggards while maintaining configuration control and maximum standardization
- managing "shirkers," or free riders.

We systematically reviewed a major selection of past attempts at global spares pooling in order to gain insights and lessons that might be applicable to the F-35. Initially, the focus was on programs with international spares pooling among foreign allies involving fighter/attack aircraft with or without U.S. participation. Because there were so few examples of pooling for fighter/attack aircraft and so little information available on the ones that exist, we expanded our search to include other types of military aircraft and concentrated primarily on European programs.

This companion report reviews other selected historical and current international military aircraft spares pooling programs involving the United States, European North Atlantic Treaty Organization (NATO) allies, or other U.S. allies. The purpose of this analysis is twofold: First, we attempt to discover whether the three risk areas identified in the main research findings regarding the F-35 spares pooling proposals were important issues of concern among the participants in historical spares pooling programs. Second, if so, we wanted to know how these concerns were mitigated or resolved in historical programs. It was hoped that such analysis might provide important historical lessons learned that could inform the final structuring the F-35 spares pooling initiative.

The comprehensiveness of the research reported in this companion document was constrained by several important factors: (1) the lack of detailed information and data available from open sources on historical cases, particularly European- or foreign-only programs, and (2) the difficulty in obtaining from any source detailed information on current and historical European- and foreign-only programs, due to a variety of national sensitivities. These challenges

---

[9] See McGarvey et al., 2015, p. xii.

were substantially increased by the fact that the historical case study research was a relatively modest component of the overall RAND F-35 spares pooling research effort in terms of personnel, funding, and time. To do a truly comprehensive examination of the historical cases would have required a very time-consuming and costly effort at trying to gain access to both U.S. and European archival military program documentation, which is difficult to track down and often very sensitive and nonreleasable. More recent programs, such as the Eurofighter Typhoon pooling effort, are difficult to access due to a variety of national sensitivities among the four partner nations, made even worse by the recent public political controversies that arose in the UK.[10]

Thus, our analysis was limited to four main sources of information: (1) open source literature, which was very sparse; (2) official government reports and parliamentary inquiries, which proved very helpful in the case of the UK Eurofighter Typhoon due to the publication of parliamentary hearings and reports by the National Accounts Office; (3) off-the-record but extensive interviews with a relatively small number of British, German, and Dutch industry and military officials involved directly in Eurofighter and NH90[11] spares pooling initiatives; and, (4) in one case (NH90), some internal documentation and briefings provided by a senior foreign military officer involved in the program negotiations.

Thus, we realize that our assessment is far from comprehensive and complete. Without detailed data, we of course cannot assess the relative success or lack thereof for any of these programs. In some cases, it is difficult to determine the precise structure and organization of the program. Nonetheless, we think we have made a valuable contribution to the overall research, for three main reasons.

1. We are unaware of any other document that comes close to this document in detailing historical and current international spares pooling initiatives, particularly foreign-only initiatives.
2. Second, we were able to confirm that at least two of the three main risks identified by the main RAND research document—(1) parts shortages and demand prioritization and (2) innovation and configuration control—were indeed major challenges in nearly all historical spares pooling initiatives we examined, with the exception of those completely dominated by one partner, such as the C-17 Global Integrated Sustainment Partnership (GISP) and F-104G.[12]
3. We also found that differing national industrial, technological, and economic objectives have historically been major barriers in programs with more equal partners, particularly all-European programs.

---

[10] See the discussion of the Eurofighter Typhoon in Chapter 2.

[11] The NH90 spares pooling negotiations are briefly reviewed in Chapter 2.

[12] The F-104G program is briefly discussed in Chapter 2. Chapter 3 includes an in-depth discussion of the C-17 GISP program.

Chapter 2 of this document reviews the historical programs RAND examined and discusses the principal reasons so few successful programs resulted from these efforts, what challenges undermined past efforts, and how these challenges and issues may inform plans for implementing F-35 global spares pooling. Chapter 3 provides greater detail on the C-17 Globemaster III Sustainment Partnership and the later C-17 GISP, one of the few largely successful current global spares programs that has extensive data available to us, in order to assess its lessons and relevance to the F-35 program.

2. NATO and European Experience with International Spares Pooling

Introduction and Overview

Given the extensive degree of intra-European and trans-Atlantic weapon system collaborative development and procurement, which has dominated European combat aircraft procurement since the 1950s, the very small numbers of successful international spares pooling programs involving major aircraft programs is surprising. Since at least the 1950s, NATO and various European defense organizations have been advocating greater collaboration among European partners in the development, procurement, and sustainment of major weapon systems. While nearly all indigenous European fighters since the early 1960s, with the important exception of the French Mirage series and Rafale fighters, have been designed, developed, and procured collaboratively, few of these fighters have established successful spares pooling support programs during their operational phases.

Since 2000, calls for greater pooling and sharing of logistics assets in Europe have increased in intensity. Several formal spares pooling initiatives have been launched by NATO and other European defense organizations, especially in the past several years, but so far few have gained traction. Only a handful of specialized small units or unique bilateral pooling arrangements have been successfully initiated. One major exception is the C-17 Strategic Airlift Capability/Heavy Airlift Wing (SAC/HAW). The C-17 SAC/HAW is part of the much larger U.S. C-17 Globemaster Sustainment Partnership/GISP program, which is examined separately in Chapter 3.

The C-17 SAC/HAW is not a fighter program, of course. The major current European collaborative fighter programs (Tornado and Eurofighter) have international spares contracts for common parts, but support is essentially a national responsibility, at least for Tornado. The Eurofighter Typhoon program began implementing an ambitious but very complex spares pooling initiative in the early 2000s, but it resulted in parts shortages for deployed Royal Air Force (RAF) aircraft and other inefficiencies. As a result, in 2012 it was replaced by an extensively restructured new support scheme, about which we have little information.

Why have there been relatively few successful European and trans-Atlantic spares pooling programs for major combat equipment programs, particularly for fighter aircraft? This chapter sheds light on that question by examining the historical record since the 1960s, with a focus on fighter aircraft.

This chapter is divided into three sections. The first section briefly reviews three major challenges that have been identified in the main RAND report as potential risk areas for USAF involvement in the proposed F-35 global spares pooling initiative. The first two of these challenges have often undermined historical attempts to establish spares pooling programs on major military aircraft programs: (1) security of supply or spares prioritization and (2) configuration control and encouragement of innovation. The third major issue, managing financial shirkers, does not appear to have been an important challenge in historical programs. These challenges were not the only ones that confronted historical programs. We focus on the first two because the case histories and analysis of historical programs and initiatives we have been able to gather—which are not always complete—clearly point to the central importance of these two challenges. Thus, examination of how past programs successfully or not-so-successfully dealt with these issues and the consequences could inform decisions for implementation strategies for F-35 pooling.

The rest of the chapter divides the historical record of European and trans-Atlantic pooling efforts initiatives into two basic periods. The first part reviews the historical record starting with the high-water mark of NATO enthusiasm for spares pooling in the 1950s and 1960s, through the decline in formal international sustainment collaboration through the 1990s. The F-104G program from the early 1960s is briefly examined as one early fighter program that included collaborative support and apparently some form of spares pooling. The F-16 international program is also briefly reviewed as a more typical case of the later period in which sustainment became a fully national responsibility.

The second half of the historical review surveys some of the major new pooling and sharing initiatives launched in Europe after 2000 and how they have fared. This period is covered separately from the earlier period because it represents a major new upsurge of interest in spares pooling approaches comparable to the earlier high-water mark of spares pooling initiatives in the 1950s and 1960s. Several specific programs from this recent period are reviewed. Information is provided on the Eurofighter spares pooling initiative, a major European effort that faced many challenges and difficulties. Other programs touched on also include the attempts to implement spares pooling on the NH90 helicopter program. All of these programs to date have achieved only partial success in implementing spares pooling.[13]

Before the historical record is examined in detail, we summarize three of the most important potential risk areas for USAF participation in the global spares sharing initiative for the F-35 as identified by the RAND overview report (McGarvey et al., 2015).

Historical Barriers to European Combat Aircraft Spares Pooling

We identified three key areas of risk for USAF participation in the global spares sharing initiative for the F-35, the first two of which were key causes of the inability of past programs to organize successful international spares pooling.

---

[13] As already noted, not enough information is available to permit an assessment of the restructured Eurofighter sustainment approach as established in 2012.

Ensuring Security of Supply

The most significant historical barrier to spares pooling, especially for fighter and other combat aircraft, is the question of *security of supply*. This issue involves the level of assurance that a partner will receive a specific part when it is needed, particularly if there is a concurrence of demand and insufficient parts are available in the pool to meet all demands. This issue is closely linked to the question of prioritization and ownership of parts and is deeply entwined with issues of national technological and industrial base policy and objectives. In European programs, it has also been historically viewed as a fundamental issue of national sovereignty and of great industrial, technological, and economic import. In many of the programs discussed in the following sections, the issue of ensuring security of supply was never satisfactorily resolved and remained one of the most important challenges undermining efforts to implement satisfactory spares pooling arrangements.

Programs that successfully dealt with this challenge often did so through the de facto mechanism of having one participant who was dominant in the program but strove to treat all partners fairly. This type of situation is illustrated by the F-104 program and the C-17 GISP program, as discussed in Chapter 3 of this report. Where no partner was dominant, this often led to increased problems and challenges, as in the case of the European Typhoon program. Without question, the issue of security of supply and prioritization has historically been the single most important challenge in European programs.

Managing Configuration Control and Encouraging Innovators

Parts commonality is a central driver of savings from spares pooling. The more parts that partner nations can share, the greater the economies of scale. Thus, it is important for partners to maintain a common aircraft configuration and to synchronize modernization efforts as much as possible. In practice, however, different national requirements and operational concepts, industrial objectives, and budgetary considerations often lead to divergent configurations, especially in the case of fighter aircraft. Therefore, a key issue in multinational spares pooling is to develop rules that promote standardization without punishing innovators and early adopters of technical modifications and improvements that may benefit other partners in the future.

As in the case of security of supply, the few programs that have successfully implemented spares pooling have often addressed this issue through the de facto mechanism of one partner dominating the configuration management, as well as innovation and upgrades. We examine two examples where this has proven successful: the F-104G fighter program and, in Chapter 3, the C-17 GISP program. In programs in which no partner was sufficiently dominant, as in the case of the European Tornado and Typhoon fighter programs, the questions of configuration control, coordinating upgrades and improvements, and not penalizing innovation have been major challenges.

7

The third major risk for USAF identified by the authors occurs when partners cannot make long-term commitments to paying their fair share of pool costs. If partners are unable or unwilling to pay their share in a given year, the additional costs may be borne by other partners. Financial shirking has been a significant challenge on some past spares pooling initiatives, particularly the questions of whether or not to punish shirkers and how to determine who is shirking, but this does not appear to have been a principle factor undermining historical attempts to pool spares. Because of a unique set of circumstances, the C-17 GISP case, as discussed in Chapter 3 of this report, has experienced major episodes of shirking, but they have not seriously hindered the program because of the program's unique characteristics.[14] It is unclear whether these circumstances are transferable or appropriate for other programs.

We now turn to the actual historical record.

Early NATO and Other European Support Cooperation and Spares Pooling Initiatives Up to 2000

Pooling spares and other defense resources is not a new concept in NATO. In response to a major U.S. initiative after the Korean War, in April 1958 the North Atlantic Council created the NATO Maintenance and Supply Organization (NAMSO), which was chartered to consolidate support activities, including pooling of spares, for any two or more NATO partners fielding the same weapon system.[15] In its heyday in the 1960s through the 1970s, when many leading European NATO nations, especially Germany,[16] fielded major U.S.-developed weapon systems produced in Europe under license, NAMSO provided pooled support services for several U.S.-developed missiles, radars, and other systems, including the Sidewinder, Hawk, and Nike missiles, which had been procured by NATO allies. However, with the one exception of the Lockheed F-104G Starfighter variant licensed produced and flown by the German, Belgian, Dutch, Italian, Turkish, Greek, and other air forces in the 1960s, NAMSO appears to have not supported a major allied fighter/attack aircraft with a comprehensive formal pooled spares program prior to the end of the 1990s. This is because the industrial and technological context in

---

[14] A potentially related question is whether instability of membership among partners involved in the program could adversely affect spares pooling programs. This is indeed an area of potential concern among some Air Force officials. However, we were unable to identify past spares pooling programs that experienced significant changes or instability of partners during implementation. Therefore, our historical research was not able to address this issue.

[15] In 2011, as part as a NATO reorganization and streamlining initiative, NAMSO became the NATO Support and Procurement Agency (NSPA).

[16] Throughout this chapter, we use *Germany* to denote the Federal Republic of Germany, colloquially referred to as West Germany during the Cold War. Of course, upon the conclusion of the Cold War, the Federal Republic of Germany absorbed the adjacent German Democratic Republic, East Germany. Today's unified Germany remains the Federal Republic of Germany.

Europe in the 1950s and early 1960s that encouraged integrated support cooperation on the F-104G began to change in later years, making implementation of spares pooling on major European fighter or other large-scale sophisticated defense programs more challenging. The early industrial and technological context is illustrated below in the discussion of the F-104G program, followed by a brief examination of the multinational F-16 program and other programs to illustrate how the context had changed by the 1970s.

The NATO European F-104G Collaborative Fighter Program

Launched in the early 1960s after a bruising and controversial international competition, the F-104G appears to be a successful early historical European fighter program that included collaborative support and a form of spares pooling. This aircraft was a significantly modified multirole variant of the USAF's F-104, which had been developed by Lockheed with little technological or industrial participation by European partners.

Detailed information on the NAMSO F-104G support effort is now difficult to find. NAMSO apparently acted principally as a common procurement agent for contract negotiations with Lockheed and foreign national licensed suppliers. Two F-104G depots were established, one in Germany supporting German, Belgian, and Dutch F-104Gs and one in southern Europe to support Italian, Turkish, and Greek F-104s. It is unclear whether NAMSO established true spares pooling for the program. There are indications that national industrial considerations were a key factor and strongly influenced how maintenance and depot-level support were undertaken by NAMSO. Most of NAMSO's support activities appear to have been related to consumables rather than spare parts and depot level repair and modifications, but we do not have sufficient information to come to any definitive conclusion.[17]

The F-104G program was typical of major European armaments programs in the late 1950s and early 1960s in that the aircraft was developed entirely by a U.S. company with little European technological developmental input and then manufactured in Europe and elsewhere under license to the U.S. contractor. The U.S. government role in the program was dominant. The F-104G variant was developed by Lockheed in the United States primarily to meet German air force requirements. The German aircraft manufacturing industries were just recovering from World War II, and they opted to retain the F-104G's basic configuration as developed by Lockheed and to focus on reestablishing their manufacturing and final assembly capabilities through licensed production of the Lockheed-designed and -modified fighter. Although Belgium, the Netherlands, Greece, Italy, and other European countries, as well as Canada, were also important partners along with Germany, they all adopted this same approach for the same reasons. The dominant role played by the U.S. government in the program was ensured by the

---

[17] For general information, see Cornell, 1981; Smith, 1986; and NATO Maintenance and Supply Organization/Agency, 2008.

9

fact that significant U.S. government financial assistance through the U.S. Military Assistance Program (MAP) funded much of the program.[18] Thus, the first 139 aircraft were manufactured and assembled by Lockheed in Burbank, California. The manufacture and final assembly of the remaining F-104Gs were then progressively moved first to Canada, where over 300 F-104Gs for the Europeans were built, then to the European partner industries in Belgium, Germany, Italy, and the Netherlands.

This situation greatly reduced the challenges of managing configuration, upgrades, and innovation. Lockheed retained all patents on the F-104G and controlled the configuration. No foreign national variants of the F-104G were developed, except for the two-seat trainer version designated the TF-104G and an insignificant number of reconnaissance versions designated RF-104G (and the later Lockheed Italian-developed F-104S discussed below). Both the TF-104G and the RF-104G were developed by Lockheed and built in the United States.

Later on, these countries moved toward development and production of specialized designs in collaboration with U.S. contractors or other European partners. For example, the Italians later collaborated with Lockheed to develop a unique national variant, the F-104S, which differed considerably from the F-104G. As Europeans moved away from U.S. military assistance programs and licensed production of U.S.-designed and developed aircraft, the problem of configuration divergence and management of spares pooling grew proportionately.[19]

According to at least one authority, NAMSO's joint support initiatives for major weapon systems declined as European national indigenous military industries, especially in Germany, revived and developed greater independent ability to design, develop, and support their own major weapon systems, particularly combat aircraft.[20] Interestingly, as the leading NATO European countries moved away from licensed-produced U.S. fighter aircraft toward collaborative European design and development of indigenous fighters, pooled spares programs and other formal joint support activities became even less common for military aircraft. Thus, the most important collaboratively developed and procured European military aircraft from the 1960s through the 1990s—including the Anglo-French Jaguar, the Franco-German Transall, the Franco-German Alpha Jet, and the Anglo-German-Italian Multi-Role Combat Aircraft (MRCA) Tornado fighter bomber—do not appear to have implemented comprehensive formal international collaborative spares pooling initiatives.

In part, this was due to the tendency to produce divergent national variants derived from differing national military requirements, greater technological and industrial capability among the participants to carry out their own sustainment and modifications on a national level, and the growth in importance of national industrial, technological, and political considerations. All these

---

[18] See Knaack, 1978.

[19] For a detailed examination of F-104 variants and production histories, see 916 Starfighter, 2014.

[20] Beer, 1969.

emerging factors in the early 1970s raised barriers to achieving successful spares pooling initiatives. For example, the French and British versions of the collaboratively designed and developed SEPECAT[21] Jaguar fighter/attack aircraft differed significantly, particularly in avionics. The British developed a substantially different air defense variant of the MRCA Tornado that differed considerably from the German attack variant. Even the British F-4K and F-4M had completely different engines and many other differences when compared with USAF F-4 Phantoms, as well as German F-4Fs.

This is also true of the most important trans-Atlantic collaborative fighter acquisition program of the era, the multinational F-16 fighter effort, which we discuss next.

The Multinational F-16 Fighter Collaborative Acquisition Program

The multinational F-16 collaborative acquisition program aimed specifically at enhancing USAF and NATO European equipment rationalization, standardization, and interoperability in order to obtain both the economic and operational benefits for the NATO alliance as a whole. The major initial partners were the U.S. Air Force and the European Participating Air Forces (EPAF) representing the Belgian, Danish, Dutch, and Norwegian air forces. Later, many other allied countries also procured the F-16. But the original program was a single consortium of the five countries aimed at manufacturing, procuring, supporting, and upgrading the aircraft in close cooperation. In many respects, the F-16 collaborative acquisition program is the most analogous historical example to the current F-35. Yet, as far as we are able to determine, international spares pooling was never even seriously considered on the F-16 program.

Based on the information available to us, we were not able to determine conclusively why this was the case. But the partners' differing industrial, budgetary, and operational objectives appear to have played an important role. If nothing else, the F-16 case clearly illustrates rapid configuration and capability divergence between the USAF and EPAF countries, even though planners originally envisioned that the Europeans would be full partners in all USAF upgrades and modifications. In 1975, the USAF and the EPAF agreed on coproduction and procurement with the F-16A/B Block 5/15 for the USAF, and mostly Block 10 and some Block 15 for the EPAF. In the early 1980s, the USAF began a major staged upgrade program explicitly designated as the Multinational Stage Improvement Program (MSIP, I-III), resulting in the F-16C/D Blocks 40/42/50/52. The EPAF, in contrast, retained the basic F-16A/B Block 10 configuration with only partial involvement in the MSIP I upgrade program to Block 15 standard.

---

[21] SEPECAT is a French acronym for the French-British joint venture company established to develop and build the Jaguar: *Société Européenne de Production de l'avion Ecole de Combat et d'Appui Tactique* (European Production Company for the Combat Trainer and Tactical Attack Aircraft).

In the early 1990s, the EPAF and the USAF agreed on a combined Mid-Life Update (MLU) program, but that update was not fully implemented. MLU was designed to partially upgrade earlier USAF and EPAF variants to Block 50 standard by upgrading the cockpit, avionics, and software. Upgraded EPAF variants would be redesignated F16A/M and B/M. Later, the USAF withdrew from this update, deciding instead to follow higher-capability options for their force structure. The EPAF cut its number of planned A/M and B/M upgrades by over 40 percent. Belgium and the Netherlands cut their total F-16 inventories by over 50 percent and 25 percent, respectively, beginning in the 1990s.

Given these significantly divergent trends on the F-16 program, one of the most collaborative U.S.-European fighter procurement programs in the postwar era, it is not surprising that spares pooling and other collaborative support initiatives were never even considered seriously on the F-16 program. Nor is it surprising that on nearly all collaboratively developed and procured European military aircraft programs up through the 1990s, where configuration management was often even more difficult, attempts at spares pooling did not succeed. A prime example is the tri-nation Tornado fighter program.

The Tri-Nation Panavia Multi-Role Combat Aircraft (MRCA) Tornado Fighter-Attack Program

The largest collaborative European fighter program of the 1970s and 1980s was the Anglo-German-Italian Panavia MRCA Tornado fighter-attack aircraft program. Panavia Aircraft GmbH is a multinational company made up of the main prime contractors of the three participating countries: British Aerospace (now BAE Systems plc), Cassidian Germany (originally MBB, then the European Aeronautic Defence and Space Company [EADS]), and Alenia Aeronautica S.p.A. (now a division of Finmeccanica).

The Tornado was collaboratively designed, developed, and procured, beginning in 1969. Development and production work allocation was contentious and politicized, leading to many inefficiencies.[22] The NATO Multirole Combat Aircraft Development and Production Management Agency (NAMMA) was the unwieldy tri-government organization that managed the tri-national aspects of the program, contracting with Panavia for airframe elements and Turbo Union for engine elements. Like Panavia, Turbo Union was a consortia of the national industries of the participating nations, in this case tasked with designing, developing, and producing the engine, the Rolls-Royce RB199.

All work shares on the program were negotiated based on procurement buys, financial contribution, and other factors (called *juste retour*, meaning that each partner had the right to

---

[22] For an excellent account of the early history of the Tornado, see Bill Gunston, "MRCA," in *Attack Aircraft of the West*, Charles Scribner's Sons, New York, 1974. Probably the most complete history of the development phase of the program from one source can be found in Alfred Mechtersheimer, *MRCA Tornado: Rüstung und Politik in der Bundesrepublik*, Osang Verlag, 1982.

receive work equivalent to its overall financial contribution and procurement buy, regardless of economic efficiencies and technological capability). There was collaborative contracting of some common parts and spares; however, a true spares pooling approach does not appear to have been established. All unique national aircraft elements including spares and much of the other support work was contracted on a purely national basis.

The only truly collaborative effort besides development and production (both of which included substantial inefficiencies due to significant national duplication of effort) was the Tri-National Tornado Training Establishment located in the UK. Interestingly, this was disbanded in the late 1990s due to in part to the continuing divergence in configuration among the three participating nations' Tornado aircraft. The national variants became so different that collaborative training made little sense, leading the partners to move all training activities back to the national level.

Indeed, one of the key challenges to spares pooling on the Tornado program was the rapid divergence in national variants. The RAF procured two distinct variants of the Tornado: the GR4 Strike/Attack Reconnaissance variant and the F3 air defense variant. The F3 variant differs significantly from the national variants procured by the other two partner nations, Germany and Italy. Italy and Germany collaborated on a midlife upgrade of their IDS (interdictor/strike) variants which included new avionics, a forward-looking infrared (FLIR) camera, and electronic countermeasures (ECM). The RAF did not take part in this program. The Germans and Italians also developed a unique ECM and reconnaissance variant of the IDS Tornado called the Tornado ECR. The RAF Tornado Air Defence Variant (ADV), or F3, accounted for approximately one-quarter of the total aircraft built for the three partners, yet it differed so dramatically from the other variants that it was practically a new aircraft. The UK and Germany also developed separate naval variants, as well as multiple types of other variants. While our evidence is not conclusive, it appears that this wide variance in national versions of the aircraft was an important reason why comprehensive spares pooling was never implemented on the program. However, it is likely that national economic, work share, and industrial base factors were equally if not more important.

By the early 2000s, it appears that the UK was conducting nearly all maintenance and support activities on RAF Tornados entirely on a national basis, in part because the main variant still in RAF service was the unique F3 air defense version. Indeed, during this period the RAF Tornado became the "poster child" for developing and implementing a new UK support policy of promoting performance-based logistics (PBL) and contractor logistics support (CLS) on a purely national basis.[23]

---

[23] For a detailed government analysis of the new logistics support approach on Tornado and Harrier, see UK National Audit Office, Report by the Comptroller and Auditor General, *Transforming Logistics Support for Fast Jets*, House of Commons 825 Sessions 2006–2007, July 17, 2007. Also see Gareth Jennings, "UK MoD Saves

Thus, configuration divergence among national variants historically has been a major impediment to comprehensive spares pooling, particularly combined with the historical tendency of partners to push their own national technological and economic agendas even at the expense of losing out on potential savings from pooling.

There were, however, one or two cases before the turn of the century when unique circumstances resulted in comprehensive spares pooling. These cases were rare, however, and so unique that their relevance to F-35 or other more traditional programs is probably minimal. The most well-known special case from this time frame that achieved success on a form of spares pooling was the NATO Airborne Early Warning and Control Program, which we discuss next. However, it is unlikely that its structure could be transferred to a major international fighter program, such as the F-35.

A Special Case: The NATO Airborne Early Warning and Control Program

One exception to the 1970s trend away from spares pooling emerged in December 1978 when, urged on by the United States government, NATO ministers approved the NATO Airborne Early Warning and Control Program (NAEW&C), which eventually included 17 NATO countries, including the United States. This program, similar to the earlier first-generation programs focusing on German rearmament, such as the European F-104G licensed production program, was a U.S.-dominated equipment procurement program. The UK and France, which, along with the Federal Republic of Germany, fielded the largest and most capable European air forces of that era, participated only as independent national partners or observers.

As originally conceived, the NAEW&C program envisioned the joint procurement, ownership, operation, and support of 18 NE-3A (variants of the Boeing E-3A AWACS aircraft). A completely separate and independent NATO bureaucracy was established for management of the program. The aircraft were based mainly in Germany, but the NATO AEW&C Program Management Organization was located in Luxembourg and reported directly to the highest levels of NATO. The aircraft are owned, operated, supported, and tasked by all partners and use multinational crews proportionately representing all partner nations for administration, operations, and support.[24] A NATO multinational logistics wing supports the aircraft.

The NATO AEW&C program has often been cited as a prime example of NATO burden-sharing and shared logistics support. However, the program is unique and was never emulated.[25] It has numerous unusual features never duplicated. First, the aircraft are not owned by any

---

Money on Tornado and Harrier Programs," *Jane's Defence Weekly*, July 19, 2007; "Tornado Maintenance Contracts Pave Way for 'Future Contracting for Availability'" *Defense Industry Daily*, December 20, 2005.

[24] All deployments and operational missions other than routine training exercises require unanimous agreement of all participating governments. The UK and French AWACS fleets determine participation on a case-by-case national basis.

[25] Attempts have been made, however. See discussion of the multirole tanker transport (MRTT) program below.

national entity, but rather by NATO as a transnational organization. Second, the U.S. government promoted the program, originally led it, and at least through 2000 paid about 40 to 50 percent of the annual cost of the program. Third, the program in some respects primarily represents a special U.S.-German bilateral arrangement promoted by the United States at the height of the Cold War. The main operational unit is based at Geilenkirchen, Germany, and has traditionally been commanded by a rotating position alternating between an American and German general officer. Perhaps most importantly, the two most significant European owners of E-3A AWACS aircraft, the UK and France, are not full members of the NATO AEW&C, with France having only observer status. The UK's seven E-3Ds and France's four E-3Fs are owned nationally, operate mainly from national bases, and are operated and supported entirely by national crews and national logistics infrastructures. UK and French participation in AEW&C operations is a national decision made on a case-by-case basis.[26] In a sense, the NATO AEW&C cannot even be viewed as a good example of spares pooling as the concept is typically understood because everything including the aircraft is pooled, and the ultimate support comes from Boeing and the USAF.

Thus, the NATO AEW&C program remains an intriguing but unique exception. Little transnational support cooperation or spares pooling has taken place on major European military aircraft programs from the 1970s through the 1990s, particularly fighter aircraft, despite years of efforts to promote cooperation. As noted earlier, after the United States helped the European national defense aerospace industries, especially German industry, to recover from World War II in the 1950s through licensed production of U.S. aircraft, international logistics initiatives for combat aircraft became increasingly rare.

Thus, throughout the 1980s and 1990s, the NATO EUROLOG Sub Group, the Western European Union (WEU), and other supranational organizations attempted to foster greater pooling of common spares and other logistics assets among NATO European partners but made little progress. Besides specific programs, such as the Tornado, NATO and the WEU also pursued a general European-wide approach to developing broad agreements that would promote greater support collaboration.

For example, there were major initiatives to achieve these goals through the signing of bilateral MoUs among officials at the highest levels of the national ministries of defense. These efforts resulted in two sets of MoUs encompassing most NATO European countries that made formal provisions for sharing support assets in emergency situations during peacetime (agreements already existed for sharing support assets in wartime). However, while these MoUs provided a formal standardized process and mechanism for spares sharing, the decision to share assets was wholly voluntary and up to the discretion of the individual lending countries involved on a case-by-case basis. In addition, the theoretical process for sharing support assets and spares

---

[26] Congressional Budget Office, 2012.

in peacetime was almost never actually followed through in reality, with the exception of a few limited events involving small deployments and exercises that took place in the early 2000s, discussed below in the next subsection.[27] The major stumbling blocks were security of supply; configuration management; and a variety of differential national technological, budgetary, and economic objectives.

More Recent European Initiatives

Recent NATO and European Union Broad Initiatives

Beginning in the early 2000s, increasing downward pressures on European defense budgets led to a revival of interest in spares pooling. A variety of initiatives led to some small successes regarding greater spares pooling to save money and at least one very ambitious attempt at spares pooling on the Eurofighter Typhoon program, which to date has had mixed outcomes. Examples of smaller efforts include Belgian-Dutch and Norwegian-Swedish bilateral spares pooling initiatives for the NH90 helicopter, as well as formal agreements among the F-16 European Partner Air Forces (EPAF, made up of the Belgian, Danish, Dutch, and Norwegian air forces) and other European F-16 owners to share spares and other support assets during joint exercise and Expeditionary Air Wing deployments. The broadest transnational initiatives that transcended specific programs emerged from two major sources: first, from the traditional NATO side from a reformed and reorganized NSPA (formerly NAMSO) and other NATO bodies, and second from the recently formed European Defense Agency (EDA) under the auspices of the European Union. While several of the most important recent initiatives technically remain within the NATO organizational context, the lead driving force behind most of them has actually been the EDA.

In July 2004, the 26 nations of the European Union (EU) established the EDA outside of NATO (thus excluding the United States). Its major objective was to promote European-wide defense industry rationalization, collaborative European weapon system development and procurement, and rationalized collaborative support of weapon systems, including spares pooling, all independent of direct U.S. oversight and influence. The catchphrase for EDA logistics reform rapidly became *pooling and sharing* (P&S).

However, the question of "security of supply" quickly emerged as the key challenge preventing greater support collaboration and spares pooling. In 2006, EDA succeeded in convincing all 26 member nations of the EU to sign a framework agreement for the sharing of defense goods and services. Yet the agreement only applied to "circumstances of operational emergency" and thus did not apply to day-to-day operations. The agreement was criticized as

---

[27] See Western European Union, 1999.

16

failing to go beyond the earlier MoUs on mutual emergency logistics support negotiated in 1984 and 1999. In short, the EDA approach failed to confront the security of supply issue for routine peacetime operations. By *security of supply*, European critics meant the assurance that national participants would receive specific parts when and where they needed them. In other words, the challenge for EDA spares pooling efforts was determining and ensuring prioritization of spares distribution, particularly when there was a correlation of demand for scarce items.[28]

In October 2010, in an attempt to resolve this issue and others, EDA asked all member ministries of defense to provide ideas and specific proposals for P&S. These proposals, submitted in December, included over 300 suggestions but generally proved disappointing to P&S advocates. Most of the proposals involved sharing of resources for training, exercises, and so forth. Very few involved specific suggestions for spares pooling, mainly because of the concerns over security of supply. In April 2011, EDA held an industry conference to review P&S approaches. Industry leaders were generally much more supportive of pooling of spares and support assets and outsourcing support tasks similar to the U.S. concept of contractor logistics support (CLS). These industry proposals, however, received a cool reception from national military and governmental organizations, mainly because of concerns over maintaining national industrial and organic logistics infrastructure and supply, as well as concerns over security of supply.[29]

At about the same time, many longer-established NATO organizations, with U.S. encouragement, began advocating similar types of programs, which often included general proposals for spares pooling. The consolidation of NAMSO and several other NATO support agencies in 2011 into the new NSPA, as part of NATO's broader reorganization and streamlining initiatives, was indicative of a more activist role in promoting P&S initiatives.

Yet very few actual programs emerged out of these theoretical discussions. Early on hopes had been raised when the F-16 EPAF countries began sharing spares on NATO Expeditionary Air Wing deployments and operational deployments to the Middle East. For example, during Exercise Cold Response 2007, the four EPAF countries plus Portugal deployed small contingents of F-16s to a Norwegian host base for a week of combined operations. A single logistics multinational ad hoc support unit was deployed along with the aircraft. Spares sharing took place, but there was no formal spares pooling. Rather, the spares were all owned by a specific nation and could be voluntarily loaned to another nation if both parties agreed, with specific payback arrangements, along the lines of the earlier NATO and EDA framework agreements on spares sharing.[30]

---

[28] Tigner, 2011.

[29] Tigner, 2011.

[30] *Defence News Defence Talk Forum,* "Will Latest F-35 Problems Push Norway Towards a European Solution?" 2008.

The two most important recent EDA P&S initiatives envisioned the joint buy of up to six MRTTs operated on the NATO AWACS model and spares pooling and other shared support activities for all the major European owners of NH90 helicopters and the Franco-German developed Tiger attack helicopters.[31] As of this writing, negotiations on spares pooling for the helicopter programs are ongoing. EDA officials envisioned the MRTT program mirroring many aspects of the NATO AWACS program, where multiple nations would jointly procure up to six MRTTs, base them at a single European location, and operate and support them with multinational crews and funding, including a single multinational depot and spares facility. This program is in its earliest stages and even if successful does not represent a classic case of spares pooling as proposed for the F-35. Like NATO AEW&C, all aspects of the program, including ownership of the aircraft, are shared on a supra-national basis.

Other programs, such as the establishment of the European Air Transport Fleet and Command, which provided for the pooling of 14 EU countries' tactical transport fleets (mainly C-130s and A400Ms), approved in November 2009 under EDA auspices, envisioned eventual spares pooling, but little progress toward that objective had been achieved at the time of this writing (April 2015). Regional pooling initiatives also gained little traction. The European Strategic Airlift Capability (SAC) Airlift Management Program (AMP) did achieve a small measure of success with three jointly owned, operated, and supported airlifters. But the European SAC AMP program does not include the major European powers and is essentially a very small component of the USAF C-17 GISP program, which is discussed in detail below in Chapter 3.

Thus, while broad top-down initiatives sponsored by trans-national organizations gained little traction, some observers hoped that specific major programs might serve as vehicles for implementing comprehensive spares pooling. The most obvious candidate was the collaborative four-nation Eurofighter Typhoon program, the largest, most expensive defense acquisition program in European history.

The Eurofighter Typhoon

The Eurofighter Typhoon is the first collaborative all-European fighter to adopt a form of spares pooling, yet it raises serious questions about the efficacy of this approach, at least as implemented on this program.

In the mid-1980s, Germany, Italy, Spain, and the UK launched the Eurofighter Typhoon program, the largest and most ambitious fighter development and procurement program ever undertaken in Europe. The four partners later agreed that maintenance and repair of the Eurofighter would be conducted on a purely national basis, but supply of spares and some equipment repair (with the exception of the engine) would be carried out through collaborative four-nation contracts that would include international spares pooling to save money.

---

[31] Tigner, 2013. See below for further information on the NH90 spares pooling initiatives.

As early as January 1997, the four partner nations formally agreed to a collaborative integrated logistics support agreement (Partner Nation Agreement Memorandum of Agreement Number 7 [MoU 7]) that would be implemented in conjunction with Production Agreement MoU 6.[32] The overall support strategy, called Typhoon Future Support, was approved in 2000 and received final approval in the 2004 Support Review. There were five basic components planned for the Typhoon Future Support strategy: Typhoon Availability Service, to be led by BAE Systems; propulsion availability service, led by Rolls-Royce; avionics spares provisioning and component repair, led by the NATO Eurofighter and Tornado Management Agency (NETMA); and international technical support, also led by NETMA.

In August 2001, the Eurofighter partners established the Eurofighter Industrial Exchange and Repair Service (IERS), which aimed at implementing comprehensive international spares pooling by 2005. NETMA awarded the original IERS contract to Eurofighter GmbH,[33] the multinational company headquartered in Munich and owned by the four participating nations' lead aerospace contractors, now called Alenia Aermacchi, BAE Systems, Cassidian Manching (Germany)[34], and Cassidian (Spain).[35]

The IERS concept envisioned a single international spares pool and component repair exchange networked to the four planned national Eurofighter main operating bases. The IERS covered 199 equipment items, divided into two categories: 60 exchange service items (remove and replace) and 139 assigned to the Guaranteed Repair Turn Round Service, which involved PBL contracts to original equipment manufacturers (OEMs) for specific equipment item repair.

In March 2003, Eurofighter GmbH opened the International Weapon System Support Centre (IWSSC) in Hallbergmoos, Germany.[36] The IWSSC represented the first formal step toward an international support organization. It included personnel from the four participating air forces, the NETMA international management agency, and Eurofighter GmbH and was intended to oversee collaborative maintenance and support for common equipment on the Eurofighter.[37]

A contract for development of a complex integrated collaborative logistics IT system software for tracking all pooled spares and repair and replace status of reparables was awarded to

---

[32] House of Commons, Public Accounts Committee, Written Evidence, *Typhoon Public Accounts Committee Hearing, Supplementary Evidence*, April 4, 2010.

[33] As noted, the Eurofighter multinational company was incorporated in Germany. GmbH is a German acronym for *Gesellschaft mit beschränkter Haftung*, translated as "limited liability corporation."

[34] Formerly European Aeronautic Defence and Space Company Deutsche Aerospace AG (EADS DASA). Cassidian is now the defense and security division of EADS.

[35] Formerly European Aeronautic Defence and Space Company Construcciones Aeronáuticas SA (EADS CASA). Cassidian is now the defense and security division of EADS.

[36] Hallbergmoos is a district of Munich near the airport near where Eurofighter GmbH and Cassidian Manching (Unterschleißheim) are located.

[37] "Vital Support Service," *Vortex Magazine: News from Eurofighter*, Issue 3, 2001. Also see David Hastings, Squadron Service, "Target Lock: Eurofighter Typhoon," last updated December 28, 2012.

BAE Systems and IFS Applications for Defence.[38] In accordance with negotiated workshare agreements, an Italian company, Züst Ambrosetti, received a contract to provide all logistics transportation services among the four main operating bases and various contractor repair centers.

In the beginning, there was considerable optimism regarding the potential for significant cost savings and greater efficiencies through the ambitious strategy of pooling spares and the use of performance-based contracting, as described above. However, the already complicated international contracting and workshare arrangements soon devolved into an even more complex and increasingly inefficient bureaucratic structure, which eventually elicited a strong critical reaction from several quarters, particularly the UK House of Commons and National Audit Office (NAO).[39]

The contentious, complex, and politically driven work-sharing arrangements negotiated on the program for the development and procurement phases of the program were applied to the support phase and undermined the implementation of an economically optimized spares pooling strategy. Eventually, 11 separate support contracts had to be negotiated for the IERS. For example, originally all four partners had aimed at maintaining the same split between organic and contractor logistics support, as well as a common maintenance approach and philosophy. Even before the final negotiation of all the IERS contracts, the partners diverged on these issues. For example, Spain pushed for a larger organic share of support than the other partners, while Germany insisted on a two-level maintenance approach, with the air force performing only flight line maintenance.[40] Later, configuration divergence and differing national equipment, upgrades, and schedules became increasingly important issues, undermining potential economies from spares pooling.

Problems with the resulting support contracts and arrangements provoked extensive criticism in the UK due to poor performance and serious shortages of spares, which negatively affected RAF readiness, particularly during operations in Libya. In March 2011, the NAO published an assessment of Typhoon program management that was critical of the international spares agreements. At about the same time, the Public Accounts Committee in the UK House of Commons held hearings on the accusations regarding spares shortages and other support problems caused by international pooling, the result of which was the publication of another highly critical report.[41]

---

[38] IFS, IFS Applications Global Marketing Brochure, *Eurofighter GmbH Case Study*, September 2006.

[39] The NAO is equivalent to the U.S. Government Accountability Office (GAO).

[40] Stewart Penney, "Eurofighter Deal Nears Signature," *Flight International*, July 2, 2001.

[41] See Comptroller and Auditor General, United Kingdom National Audit Office, *Ministry of Defence: Management of the Typhoon Project,* HC 755 Session 2010–2011, London, HMSO, March 2, 2011; and House of Commons, Committee of Public Accounts, *Management of the Typhoon Project*, Thirteenth Report of Session 2010–2012, London, HMSO, April 15, 2011.

Both the NAO and House of Commons investigations and reports found that the international spares pooling contracts for Eurofighter were not working well. According to these studies, the international spares pooling contracts led to significant shortages of spares for the RAF Typhoons, negatively affecting readiness and availability rates. Some press reports claimed that these spares shortages led to a reduction in Typhoon readiness and availability rates during combat operations in Libya after RAF Typhoons had deployed to forward operating bases in Italy.[42] We were not able to confirm whether these allegations were accurate, but there is no doubt that the international spares pooling contracts did not contain sufficient incentives for contractor performance, particularly during surges, and that the RAF was experiencing serious spares shortages for its Eurofighters as a result, at least according to credible government reports. Furthermore, the reports made clear that no such problems were experienced on the UK national spares support contracts that supported the equipment and parts on UK Eurofighters that were unique to the UK variants.[43]

This issue led directly to the complete renegotiation of the international cooperative spares contracts in 2012. The existing 11 support contracts were consolidated down to four contracts. It also appears that the new contracts represent a major move toward greater PBL and CLS, pushed very strongly by the UK. In March 2012, NETMA awarded a new five-year contract to the Eurofighter international consortium (AleniaAermacchi in Italy, BAE Systems in the United Kingdom, and Cassidian in Germany and Spain) for engineering support and other technical and logistical support services for the Eurofighter fleets in Germany, Italy, Spain, and the United Kingdom.[44] However, it is not clear whether the new contracts include comprehensive spares pooling and, if so, how the policy is structured. Furthermore, the specific national support relationships appear to have been negotiated on a national basis directly between each partner national government and its own lead national industry partner, with a careful eye to *juste retour* and the original work-sharing agreements based on procurement buy. We were unable to obtain sufficient information on the new contracts to determine their exact nature. What remains clear is that the original spares pooling contracts were found to be severely deficient, at least according

---

[42] For example, see BBC News, "RAF Typhoon Jets Grounded Owing to Spares Shortages," April 15, 2011; Ian Drury, "RAF Strips Jets for Spare Parts: Typhoons Torn Up for Libya Air Fleet," *Daily Mail,* June 16, 2011; and Marco Giannangeli, "RAF Hit by Crisis Over Spares for Fighter Jets: Nearly Half the RAF's New Typhoon Jets Are Grounded Because of Maintenance and Lack of Spare Parts," *The Daily Express*, December 4, 2011.

[43] We queried a senior Typhoon industry logistics official regarding these UK government reports and press allegations. This official claimed that the UK situation was more "subtle" than reported in the press and in government reports because the UK MoD allegedly "spent much less" on spares than the other partners but flew more hours, thus resulting in a net benefit to the UK. To date no detailed information has yet been provided to back up these claims. In addition, even if true, this outcome does not necessarily indicate that Eurofighter spares pooling was a net benefit and cost saver for the other partners or contradict the assertions made by government reports that RAF Typhoon readiness levels fell below desirable levels due to the spares pooling contracts.

[44] "Eurofighter Receives Typhoon Support Contract From NETMA," *Airforce Technology*, April 2, 2012.

to several UK government reports, and led to spares shortages that may have directly affected readiness rates during combat deployments.

The problems encountered on the Eurofighter spares pooling program may also have had an effect on other major programs, such as the NH90. This program, one of the largest collaborative European military aircraft programs ever undertaken in Europe, struggled for many years unsuccessfully to implement a spares pooling strategy to save O&S costs. A brief review of those attempts, provided next, underscores the common thread of similar challenges that ran through all the European spares pooling initiatives from the late 1990s to the present.

The NH90 Medium Helicopter

The NH90 medium helicopter program is one of the largest current European collaborative military acquisition programs. Launched in 1992, the NH90 program included France, Germany, Italy, and the Netherlands in the collaborative development and production of the helicopter intended for both army and naval forces. Portugal joined the original four partners in June 2001. The program was managed by a complex five-nation NATO organization called the NATO Helicopter Management Agency (NAHEMA) and was developed and produced by an international consortium called NHIndustries made up of EADS Eurocopter (itself a collaborative international European company), Augusta Westland, and Fokker. After many delays, the first production helicopter was delivered in late 2006. Portugal began negotiations for withdrawal from the program in 2012 before receiving its helicopters, but eventually at least 13 nations, including the four remaining initial partners and several other European countries, committed to buying the aircraft.[45] While the original program did not envision it, both binational and broader European programwide spares pooling initiatives were launched as the helicopter entered into production.

The major effort launched in the early 2000s at achieving a genuine pooled spares support approach for nationally procured and owned NH90 helicopters is an instructive case for the F-35, since we have more information on the precise details of the challenges confronting spares pooling on this program than on Eurofighter and other European programs.

Belgium, which signed a contract for eight aircraft in 2007, soon thereafter entered into bilateral negotiations with the Netherlands (which had ordered 20 NH90s) for cooperative support of the aircraft, including spares pooling. The negotiations were conducted within the framework of a broader strategic bilateral defense cooperation agreement signed by Belgium and the Netherlands in 1995 called the BENESAM Accord. Nonetheless, despite the special Belgian-

---

[45] The UK had been an early member but withdrew in 1987 before the initial contracts were signed. Finland, Greece, Italy, Norway, Portugal, Spain, and Sweden later joined the program. Non-European participants included Australia, New Zealand, Oman, and Saudi Arabia, although Saudi Arabia cancelled its order in October 2007. For more details, see "NH90: Europe's Medium Helicopter Contender," *Defense Industry Daily*, August 5, 2013, and Tony Osborne, "NH90 Faces Up to European Budget Cuts," *Aviation Week and Space Technology*, June 17, 2013.

Dutch relationship, the negotiations progressed very slowly. After years of negotiating, the two partners agreed in principle to eventually concentrate most depot level work at a single Dutch facility and begin slowly phasing in parts pooling by starting with the engine only.[46] However, this has not yet actually happened as of April 2015.

Belgium and the Netherlands initiated these discussions bilaterally on their own initiative, mainly for the purpose of reducing support costs for their very small fleets through spares pooling. However, EDA and European NATO officials quickly piggybacked on this effort and pushed strongly for the larger NH90 countries, especially France and Germany, to join and formalize the pooled logistics approach under negotiation by Belgium and the Netherlands to form a much broader European-wide NH90 spares pooling effort.

Formal NH90 programwide negotiations began at various NATO locations shortly after the beginning of the Belgian-Dutch bilateral effort, but they progressed slowly. After several years of negotiations, the participants finally developed a five-tiered theoretical framework of differing levels of participation in spares pooling and other logistics sharing on the NH90 program, but nothing to date has actually been implemented (as of April 2015).

The formal theoretical levels of participation negotiated by the participants spanned the spectrum from voluntary sharing along the lines of the Mutual Emergency Logistics Support MoUs from 1984 and 1999 and the later 2006 EDA P&S sharing framework initiative up to the highest level, including a mutual common physical stock stored at a central location, non-national ownership of the pooled spares, and full visibility into the stock positions, consumption, and resupply situations of each national partner. This maximal position was the formal stated objective of the French, German, Dutch, and Belgian negotiating partners. However, as of early 2013, none of the partners had agreed on any of the basic details of such a pooled spares approach to supporting the NH90, including common spares stock definition, the role played by NAMSA and the NATO Helicopter Management Agency, cost-sharing, and configuration management.[47]

Thus, as of this writing, the NH90 program continues to struggle with many of the same types of challenges that have bedeviled European attempts to establish successful comprehensive spares pooling programs over the past five decades. The early post–World War II era represented a golden age in transatlantic collaborative acquisition and cooperative sustainment, mainly because of the widespread devastation of much of Europe's aeronautical industrial infrastructure, limited European national financial resources, and the unquestioned political, technological, and industrial leadership position of the United States. Thus, successful pooling programs, such as

---

[46] Interview, senior Belgian Air Force officer, May 2013. Norway and Sweden are also investigating spares pooling for their NH90s.

[47] NATO Helicopter Management Agency, 2013a and 2013b.

the F-104G, were launched, but they were based on licensed production of U.S.-designed and -developed equipment and were dependent on U.S. leadership and subsidies.

Once the European aeronautical industry reconstituted, the larger European countries moved away from dependency on U.S. programs and designs. Yet for major programs, the Europeans were driven to cooperate among themselves in order to pool their limited resources. For many decades, however, differing European national economic and technological objectives made full cooperation, especially in the area of spares pooling, difficult to achieve. Even when relatively small partners, such as the EPAF countries, teamed with the United States, national industrial interests tended to trump economic efficiency goals, making spares pooling and collaborative sustainment difficult to achieve.

It is only in the last decade that the Europeans have seriously turned back toward a stronger commitment to achieving cost savings through international spares pooling among themselves. With no dominant partner playing an undisputed leadership role, as in the case of the United States in the 1950s and 1960s, implementing successful pooling initiatives remained a challenge. Some successes have been achieved, however. The Eurofighter Typhoon program appears to have made a major effort toward pooling spares beginning in 2003. The data necessary for fully assessing these more recent programs are not readily available, so it is difficult to know how well they have performed. There is at least some evidence, however, as in the case of the original Eurofighter sustainment contracts, that many wrinkles remain to be ironed out.[48]

In short, the European experience with spares pooling and collaborative sustainment for major combat aircraft programs over the last half century has been limited, and the success of the few programs that have been established remains uncertain. There is at least one successful international pooling program that appears to be relatively successful and for which data are available. This program is the C-17 GISP. We examine this program in the next chapter to seek lessons applicable to the F-35.

---

[48] Phone discussion with senior Typhoon industry logistics official, October 2013.

3. The C-17 Global Integrated Sustainment Partnership

The C-17 GISP program is the only truly successful ongoing international military aircraft support program using true spares pooling for which we have any detailed and reliable data, and it is the closest current analogy to the proposed F-35 global spares pooling program. This chapter summarizes the C-17 GISP program and examines the role played in that program by the three key issues identified in the RAND assessment of the F-35 pooling proposal.

Overview of the C-17 GISP

The C-17 GISP is a comprehensive long-term sustainment and support contract between the USAF and Boeing.[49] It is a modified CLS contract using a performance-based logistics (PBL) approach. Boeing is responsible for all C-17 sustainment activities (other than organizational-level maintenance), including supply support, supplier management, technical manual support, maintenance, modifications and upgrades, logistics engineering services, and field support services. Boeing is responsible for supply support management for more than 95 percent of the reparable parts on the C-17.

Boeing has full wholesale accountability for all C-17 unique spares and engine spares (labeled F77 spares). This amounts to about 60 to 70 percent of total C-17 spares by parts number and about 90 percent or more of spares by total cost. The company fully manages the supply chain, spares stockage, spares storage, and spares distribution for all F77 spares. The remaining non-C-17 unique spares are managed by the Defense Logistics Agency and the Air Force Air Logistics Centers.[50]

All FMS customers who own the C-17 are members of GISP. Support of the foreign C-17s is carried out under the virtual fleet (VF) support concept. This means that, in effect, all foreign C-17s are treated as indistinguishable from any other C-17. In other words, the VF support concept assumes there is only one fleet of nearly identical C-17s, which happens to include all USAF C-17s and C-17s from a variety of foreign air forces. All the C-17s in the single VF are treated according to the same contractual rules and regulations, no matter who owns them.

Two key characteristics of the spares pool facilitate Boeing's transfer of spares and components to and from foreign partners in the VF. First, the USAF owns all pooled spares and

---

[49] This description is based on open source documentation; PAF interviews with senior government and Boeing officials at the C-17 GISP Combined Program Office (CPO) located at Robins Air Force Base, Georgia; and releasable information from CPO internal documents and briefings.

[50] U.S. government regulatory policy prevents Boeing from managing spares and other parts that are common to more than one aircraft.

components handled by Boeing until a part is actually installed on a foreign aircraft. Any part or component pulled off a foreign aircraft by Boeing returns immediately to USAF ownership. These rules apply even if the spares are stored and the FMS aircraft are on a foreign base in the foreign country. Second, Boeing is the sole importer and exporter of record of C-17 F77 parts and operates under authority of a Department of State DSP-5 export license for the export of unclassified technical data. Thus, technically, a part is not exported until it is installed on an FMS aircraft. This facilitates Boeing's optimal management of pooled spares that can be stored anywhere in the world at U.S. or FMS customer bases, since the spares remain U.S.-owned and controlled by Boeing until they are actually installed in an aircraft. Thus, Boeing can provide a part needed for any C-17 located anywhere in the world and owned by any participating country from any location, foreign or domestic, where F77 parts are stored, without going through a complex set of U.S. government export control regulations for each parts transfer. According to the CPO, this was an extremely important lesson learned early on in the program.

Boeing determines appropriate spares storage locations and stockage levels based on a variety of contractual incentives. Since GISP is a modified PBL CLS contract, participants, including the foreign partners, buy a service from Boeing to maintain a variety of fleetwide readiness metrics, such as quick response to repairing non–mission-capable aircraft (mission-impaired capability awaiting parts [MICAP]) and other performance metrics, across the entire VF.

Participants pay in proportion to estimated annual total flying hours, engine cycles, and a variety of other metrics. The contract and its incentive structure have evolved over the years, including two main phases. The USAF adopted a system-level performance-based contract approach in 1998, before there were any FMS aircraft. In 2003, the USAF negotiated the C-17 Globemaster III Sustainment Partnership, making Boeing the C-17 product support integrator lead, with total system support responsibility. At this time there was only one FMS customer, the UK.[51] This was an indefinite-delivery, indefinite-quantity contract with a fixed-price component for labor and cost-plus component for materiel, and it was a one-year contract with four priced annual options. At the end of five years, the USAF awarded Boeing a three-year extension.

In 2011, the contract was renegotiated and revamped, becoming the C-17 GISP. The major difference was that the USAF retained more oversight and management authority than under the earlier contract. The Air Force Air Logistics Center at Warner Robins Air Force Base became the C-17 product support integrator lead instead of Boeing. Several aspects of the contract, including incentives, were altered and refined, but the basic contract structure remained largely the same. By this time, there were seven FMS partners and members of the C-17 VF: the United Kingdom (eight aircraft), Australia (six aircraft), Canada (four aircraft), Qatar (four aircraft), the United Arab Emirates (six aircraft), India (ten aircraft with an option for six more), and the NATO SAC

---

[51] At this point the UK was actually leasing its C-17s.

AMP consortium (three aircraft). As of May 2013, a total of 254 C-17s had been delivered. Of these, 220 were owned by the USAF, and 32 were owned by FMS customers.[52]

The NATO SAC AMP consortium discussed above agreed to join the C-17 Globemaster Sustainment Partnership in 2008. NATO signed an MoU with Boeing for the FMS purchase of two C-17s by the NATO Airlift Management Agency (NAMA), while the USAF agreed to provide a third. NAMA then joined the Globemaster Sustainment Partnership to provide all maintenance and support.[53]

The remainder of this chapter examines how the C-17 Globemaster Sustainment Partnership/GISP program has dealt with challenges identified for the F-35 spares pooling proposal.

Configuration Management and Promoting Innovation

As discussed in Chapter 2, the problem of maintaining a common configuration to obtain full savings from economies of scale in spares pooling programs has been a major stumbling block in past efforts to establish spares pooling. This has been particularly true in European collaborative fighter/attack procurement programs, where national partner configurations tended to diverge rapidly, thus reducing the economic incentives for spares pooling.

The C-17 Globemaster Sustainment Partnership/GISP program recognized the crucial importance of configuration management and control to maintain maximum commonality from the beginning of the program. In addition, the C-17 GISP program sought to reward rather than punish innovators and partners who quickly adopted innovations developed by the innovation leader, which was nearly always the USAF.

When the UK became the first foreign partner to join the program, the RAF sought only four aircraft and intended to lease rather than buy in anticipation of later receiving the European collaboratively developed A400M military transport, whose development had been delayed. Announced initially in May 2000, the lease terms provided the RAF with an option to purchase their four C-17s with favorable terms. However, to obtain this option, the RAF had to agree to upgrade their C-17s in line with the USAF and to maintain 100-percent commonality with USAF versions. The RAF decided to exercise their purchase option in 2004, after the negotiation of the original USAF C-17 Globemaster Sustainment Partnership support contract with Boeing. This experience established the precedent and demonstrated the benefits to both parties of maintaining maximum commonality to achieve maximum economic benefits from pooled spares and common support approaches.

---

[52] One delivered USAF C-17 was retired, and one was destroyed in a Class A mishap.

[53] An excellent published summary of the C-17 Globemaster Sustainment Partnership/GISP program can be found in *Defense Industry Daily*, "The Global C-17 Sustainment Partnership," January 17, 2013.

Later, when other foreign partners bought the C-17, it became clear that supporting very small fleets of C-17s separate from the Globemaster Sustainment Partnership/GISP program would be prohibitively expensive for the FMS customer, and membership in Globemaster Sustainment Partnership/GISP from the USAF's perspective required maximum configuration commonality to achieve maximum economic benefits. The USAF encouraged configuration commonality in three ways. First, it required FMS partners to pay only for the recurring costs of modifications and upgrades required by the USAF, but not nonrecurring costs. Secondly, it heavily incentivized Boeing to standardize the existing number of C-17 blocks during depot-level maintenance from five down to two very similar blocks. As equal members of the VFs, foreign-owned C-17s would be subject to the same incentives and treatment as USAF C-17s with respect to depot modifications. Finally, the basic economics of maintaining very small aircraft fleets (every foreign partner prior to India maintained single-digit fleets) outside of the Globemaster Sustainment Partnership/GISP context would be prohibitively expensive, since the contract stipulated no shared support costs for the nonstandard parts of national unique versions that differed from USAF versions as the baseline.

Concerned about the cost of the requirement to adopt all USAF modifications whether desired or not, two FMS partners commissioned an independent study that looked at the cost and benefits of paying for upgrading and modifying their C-17s to USAF standards, even if the modifications and upgrades were not a foreign national requirement, compared to the savings obtainable by refusing to undertake unwanted USAF upgrades and modifications. The study determined that it was cheaper to pay for maintaining maximum commonality with the USAF baseline even though unwanted upgrades and improvements had to be paid for. This, of course, was because maintenance of nonstandard aspects of FMS C-17s would require negotiation of a separate national support agreement with the contractor that would likely be extremely expensive due to the very small size of the individual FMS fleets.

The real leverage exercised by the USAF was the disproportionate size of the various national fleets. Whereas the USAF deployed 220 aircraft, the foreign partners fielded only very small single-digit fleets and had no major industrial participation in the program. Thus, all the economic and technological leverage remained with the USAF and its negotiated agreements with Boeing. Like the F-104, the C-17 was developed exclusively for the USAF, with no foreign participation in the requirements, design, and development processes.

Military transport aircraft, such as the C-17, have fairly straightforward missions and tactical operational employment concepts in most air forces. However, doctrine, roles, and missions for fighter aircraft can vary considerably in different national air forces. This is another reason that the common configurations of collaboratively developed and procured fighter aircraft have historically been more difficult to achieve. Add to this the trend toward continuing divergence in configuration even among the three participating U.S. services, and the following conclusions are likely: A common configuration among participants in the F-35 program will be much more difficult to maintain than on the C-17 program. In addition, the USAF and Lockheed will not have nearly the leverage to impose conformity with U.S. configurations on the F-35 program FMS partners compared to the C-17 program because of the more equal fleet sizes, the much larger divergence already existing among U.S. variants, and the much greater economic and industrial participation of the F-35 partners in the development and production and sustainment programs.[54]

Security of Supply: Prioritization and Allocation of Scarce Resources

As noted in Chapter 2 in the discussions of various historical European programs, one of the most significant barriers to spares pooling, especially for fighter and other combat aircraft, is the question of security of supply. Simply put, this issue involves the level of assurance that a partner will receive a specific part when it is needed, particularly if there is a concurrence of demand and insufficient parts are available in the pool to meet all demands. This issue is closely linked to the question of prioritization and ownership of parts. In Europe, it is also viewed as a fundamental issue of national sovereignty and of great industrial, technological, and economic import.

Prioritization and security of supply have been major issues on the C-17 Globemaster Sustainment Partnership/GISP program, but years of experience have led to what the program office argues is a satisfactory solution. According the C-17 GISP officials, security of supply is no longer an important issue on the program. The question of interest is whether the solutions developed by the C-17 GISP program can shed light on the important challenge for the proposed F-35 pooling effort.

The key elements of the C-17 GISP program in this area are as follows: First, and most important, all C-17s, both USAF and FMS, are treated the same as equal members of the C-17 GISP global virtual fleet. Boeing, as the recipient of a modified CLS PBL contract, has been incentivized by the contract to meet and exceed a variety of readiness and performance metrics across the entire VF in order to receive its full contractual award fee.[55] Ideally, Boeing as the CLS contractor must service and support the aircraft in a "nationality-blind" manner. Boeing operates under a formula encompassing multiple performance metrics, but two of the most important are fleet performance aircraft availability (FPAA) and responsiveness to MICAPs. FPAA is weighted for meeting overall Boeing performance goals for the purpose of determining

---

[54] For example, F-35 foreign partners are projected to have large fleets relative to the United States (FMS/US %), particularly for some variants, such as STOVL (57%) and CTOL (30%) compared to the C-17 GISP (14% up to 20%). Three foreign F-35 partners will conduct full national final assembly and check out (FACO) on their own national territory. The UK and several other partners invested heavily in development of the F-35 and influenced the requirements and design. (Based on data from the December 2010 F-35 Selected Acquisition Report.)

[55] More precisely, there are seven metrics directly linked to the contractor's incentive fee and nine additional contractual metrics that are not linked to the incentive fee.

the incentive fee award, and is stated as a single number. This metric applies to the entire VF, including all USAF and FMS aircraft.

MICAP aircraft always have the highest priority. MICAP responsiveness is measured against a specific number of hours Boeing needs to transfer a part to a U.S. base or, for FMS partners, to an authorized shipper to send out the part.

The original Globemaster Sustainment Partnership contract first negotiated in 2003 led to some dissatisfaction among FMS customers regarding the calculation of the FPAA and MICAP metric. There were two problems. In the Globemaster Sustainment Partnership contract, the metrics were only calculated once every six months. This permitted the contractor to smooth out overall performance over a relatively long period of time and thus mask poor performance during a small number of months with high performance for a majority of months in the period. Furthermore, with the vast bulk of the aircraft owned by the USAF, the contractor tended to focus on achieving and surpassing the metric for USAF aircraft, sometimes at the expense of FMS aircraft. High performance for the USAF aircraft would more than offset poor performance on a small number of FMS aircraft. However, this issue was most problematic with MICAPs. In the Globemaster Sustainment Partnership contract, USAF and FMS MICAPs were folded into the same metric. A high response rate for USAF aircraft would easily cancel out a very poor performance rate for FMS aircraft. This is of course because if Boeing performed very well with respect to mitigating MICAPs for the USAF but performed poorly for the FMS fleets, the *average* performance across the entire fleet of USAF plus FMS aircraft could still be high enough to meet the MICAP metric because the USAF fleet was so much larger than all the FMS fleets combined.[56]

Two major reforms were instituted in the GISP contract to remedy these issues. The first was that the calculation and award of the incentive fee was changed from once every six months to once every month. This made it much more difficult for the contractor to smooth out poor performance on one or two months with superior performance over the several remaining months. This may also have discouraged any preference shown to USAF aircraft compared to FMS aircraft, again because of the shorter time period and greater difficulty in smoothing out the data.

Even more important from the FMS owners' perspective, MICAP responsiveness was broken out into two separate metrics equally weighted, one for USAF responsiveness and one for FMS aircraft responsiveness. Indeed, according to the program office, this has had the effect of incentivizing the contractor to place the highest priority on FMS MICAP responsiveness because, with the small FMS fleets, just one shortfall represents a much higher percentage

---

[56] This is not to suggest that Boeing necessarily showed a conscious preference for repairing USAF MICAPs rather than those for other nations; if Boeing simply addressed MICAPs in the order that they arrived, a smaller partner with four aircraft that had one MICAP waiting in the queue would have a 25 percent MICAP rate at that point in time.

MICAP rate for the whole FMS fleet than one shortfall in MICAP responsiveness for the much larger USAF fleet.

MICAPs always have the highest priority, but the C-17 GISP program does not have explicit written rules on prioritization in the case of concurrence of demand within the same category for scarce spare parts. Program officials insist that there have been very few, if any, instances when this situation has arisen. When pressed on what would theoretically happen if such a situation arose, particularly when concurrence in demand for MICAPs existed between a USAF and FMS C-17, program officials claimed that the operational commander would decide based on mission priorities. Yet the question remains: Who is the operational commander if there is a conflicting need for the same scarce part between a foreign-based FMS aircraft and a locally based USAF aircraft? While we were not provided with a definitive answer, it appears that the senior operational C-17 command, the USAF Air Mobility Command (AMC), would make the final decision on prioritization in a situation of concurrence of demand.

One interesting element of the GISP contract is that it is divided into two major parts: a fixed-price element for labor and a cost-plus element for materiel. The contractor, in conjunction with the USAF, using sophisticated modeling tools and past data, determines both stockage levels for the F77 parts and storage locations for the parts, whether in the United States or on foreign bases overseas.[57] The purpose is to optimize availability and minimize delivery time for spares to wherever they are needed. The contract also holds the contractor responsible for achieving the same performance metrics, even under conditions of unplanned surges. The contractor is permitted to purchase extra spares to cover such contingency situations. The fact that the material contract is cost-plus and the contractor's incentive fee is heavily dependent on meeting and surpassing performance metrics, even under surge conditions, would suggest that the contractor may be incentivized to be conservative in calculating overall spares requirements (i.e., the contractor would want to purchase a large number of spare parts), thus reducing theoretical economic benefits of pooling.

The apparent success of the GISP contract in handling the security of supply and prioritization issues of scarce spares may at least in part still be a function of the overwhelming dominance of the USAF component in the virtual fleet compared to any FMS participant. As noted earlier, no foreign partner is currently committed to purchasing more than ten aircraft, and most deploy only very small single-digit fleets. In addition, none of the FMS partners has any formal industrial participation in the program. Not surprisingly, the USAF, with 220 aircraft, completely dominates the program and ultimately determines contract parameters and spares stockage and prioritization of demand along with the contractor.

---

[57] There are 12 USAF bases and seven foreign air force bases on which spare parts are stored. Of course, parts can be taken from any U.S. or any foreign location and moved anywhere else when needed.

Financial Shirking

Finally the issue of shirking—the situation in which a partner is unable or unwilling to pay its allocated share of the cost of spares pooling—and how this affects the other partners was identified as a major potential risk for USAF participation in the F-35 spares pooling initiative. We sought to learn whether this issue arose on the C-17 program and how it was mitigated.

We were unable to obtain detailed information on the prevalence and effects of financial shirking on the C-17 GISP program. However, based on available information and our interviews with program officials, several important points can be made. Shirking among FMS partners apparently has not been a common problem, and if it did take place, it would have little overall effect on the program. Again, this is because of the dominance of the large numbers of USAF aircraft in the VF and the very small size of each of the FMS partner fleets. There were apparently at least one or two incidents when shirking took place, but in these cases the shirker was the USAF. This was due to major funding cut backs mandated by the executive branch and Congress requiring a cutback in either flying hours or spares purchases, which in turn would affect readiness rates. The determination of the effects of this shirking, however, is complex. This is because of the two different types of contracts used on the program, the fixed-price contract for labor and the cost-plus contract for materiel. Allocated labor costs are based on fixed-price annual prepriced options paid up front and based on planned flying hours. All partners contract at the same FPAA rate and the same MICAP metrics, and the pool is funded based on flying hours and engine cycles, in which each participant pays in accordance with the share of its expected flying hours and engine cycles of the total for the entire VF. Because of budgetary cuts, the USAF had to significantly cut flying hours and engine cycles, increasing the relative share of total flying hours and engine cycles for the FMS partners. While the precise mechanism remains unclear, this situation resulted in the same or reduced costs for the FMS partners because they had already signed fixed-price labor agreements. In effect, the fixed-price cost labor rates had already been paid based on predicted flying hours. However, the USAF also sought to save money by lowering overall readiness rates through decreased purchases of spares, which is a cost-plus contract. Here, too, the FMS partners experienced reduced costs but also reduced readiness rates because the metrics for the entire VF must always remain the same for all partners. Thus, when the USAF cut back on FPAA rates to save spares costs, all FMS partners had to accept the reduced rates but also paid less.

This situation works for the C-17 GISP again because of the very small size of the FMS fleets compared to the USAF fleet. It is unlikely that this approach would work on the F-35 program. This is particularly true because a major cutback from a large foreign partner could have significant effects on the USAF, a situation that is very unlikely in the C-17 GISP program.

In addition, there is some evidence that shirking has been a serious challenge on other U.S. programs, based on our discussions with USAF officials. One such program involved a pooled engineering support contract, which included the USAF and over 20 foreign partners. This was an annual contract with options similar to C-17 GISP. Routinely, one or more of the foreign partners would experience budget problems near the finalization of the contract, which would cause serious disruption to the program. Usually the shirker was relatively small and owed a relatively small sum compared to the USAF and some other larger partners. Typically the USAF and other partners sought to "cover" temporarily for the shirker, assuming later payback. However, this approach proved very challenging in practice because there was no formal mechanism by which this solution could be implemented. Thus the shirking on this program caused, at a minimum, significant delays for the USAF and other partners in finalizing the contract and moving forward with the program's support services.

In short, once again the unique nature of the C-17 GISP program, with the heavy preponderance of influence exercised by the USAF and the small fleets of the partner nations, led to few significant problems from shirking. However, based on the experience of other U.S. programs, such as the one mentioned above, shirking can result in contracting delays and other modest challenges. Those challenges might be greater if partners were more equal in fleet size and financial contribution, as in the case of the F-35 pooling proposal.

It is evident from this assessment that the C-17 GISP program is a generally successful and genuinely innovative attempt to implement comprehensive international spares pooling. It has benefited from ten years of trial and error dating back to the early 2000s and clearly offers important lessons for other similar efforts. The program appears to have developed mechanisms to cope with three of the potentially most important risks identified by RAND posed by the F-35 spares pooling proposal. However, our assessment indicates that many lessons from the C-17 GISP program may not be directly applicable to the F-35 program because that program differs considerably, as discussed throughout this chapter.

4. Conclusions

Our review of NATO and European attempts to implement comprehensive spares pooling initiatives and programs since the 1960s reveals that the results have been modest at best. The F-104G fighter program and other major defense programs achieved some success in the 1950s and 1960s, but these programs were dominated by the United States and entailed licensed production of U.S. designed and developed systems. Once European national industries fully recovered from the destruction of World War II, the leading European powers rejected licensed production of U.S. systems and sought to collaboratively develop indigenous systems. Most of the codeveloped and coproduced systems did not include pooled spares initiatives because of nationalistic economic, industrial, and technological factors.

However, with the steep decline in defense budgets after the end of the Cold War, and particularly after 2000, European interest in spares pooling as a means to reduce costs for expensive systems, such as Eurofighter and NH90, surged. Yet none of the major initiatives has led to fully satisfactory programs. Most initiatives have stalled. The largest spares pooling effort, launched in 2003 for Eurofighter, resulted in major challenges, including spares shortages and poor readiness rates, which ultimately led to the restructuring and renegotiation of the entire program in 2012.

The only clear European and trans-Atlantic successes to date appear to be programs in which most of the international partners had very little stake in the design and development stages, one partner subsidized the program, and that partner exercised clear technological, financial, and economic leverage. This was true in the 1950s and early 1960s, as well as more recently.

The most obvious current example is the C-17 GISP program. This spares pooling initiative is generally considered to be a success. Yet this program differs from the F-35 global spares proposal in important ways. A key attribute of the C-17 GISP program is that foreign partners do not have major design and industrial stakes in the development and production of the aircraft; moreover, their fleets are relatively small. Thus, the USAF is able to maintain common configuration by requiring all partners to make all of the upgrades and modifications that the USAF undertakes. This is because the support cost benefits that accrue to the allied partners far outweigh the extra cost of modifying aircraft to meet the USAF standard and configuration. In case of parts shortages, the USAF's Air Mobility Command exercises the authority to allocate scarce resources. Financial shirking has not been a problem because the foreign partner fleets are small.

In contrast, the F-35 partner nations have major design and industrial stakes in the development and production of the aircraft, and the disparity in fleet size is much lower than for the C-17. Thus, it is not surprising that under the draft business rules for F-35 spares sharing, no U.S. service has primacy over allocation decisions for scarce spares and no U.S. service controls configuration management. Therefore, any F-35 spares pooling initiative is likely to look much more like previous collaborative efforts, such as Eurofighter, which to date have not led to satisfactory spares pooling programs, than like the C-17.

Our analysis shows that while several attempts at asset-pooling programs have been made, international spares pooling programs are rare and difficult to implement, especially for fighters and other combat aircraft. We were unable to identify any major successful historical fighter/attack aircraft programs from recent decades that led to formal global spares pooling, with the possible exception of the Eurofighter Typhoon, which has been subject to extensive government criticism in the UK. Thus, the F-35 will be the first program we are aware of aimed at implementing spares pooling with the primary focus, at least from the USAF side, on economic efficiency and cost savings. Most past historical attempts have foundered on the challenges of security of supply (demand prioritization), configuration control and encouraging innovators versus laggards, and national industrial base concerns, as well as other issues. A successful F-35 spares pooling program must carefully review these issues and develop comprehensive strategies for dealing with them to avoid a similar fate.

In summary, our assessment of historical cases of international spares pooling resulted in the following high-level findings:

- Historically, the negotiation of international spares pooling programs for common major weapon systems has been attempted many times since the 1960s but has proven to be very difficult to implement. There are far more failures than successes.
- We found three major historical barriers to the successful negotiation of spares pooling programs in the past. The first two were similar to the first two risk areas identified in the principal RAND report: (1) security of supply and prioritization of scarce spares assets and (2) configuration management and managing innovators versus laggards. These two challenges can be difficult to overcome unless one partner plays a dominant role in the pooling arrangements.
- Shirking did not appear to have been a critical problem on past programs.
- A major historical challenge, especially for all-European programs or programs in which all the partners were roughly of equivalent size and influence, was conflicting industrial, technological, and economic interests and objectives.
- The most successful historical programs were characterized by a single dominant partner who could establish the ground rules and resource allocation priorities, as well as control configuration. At the same time, successful programs made major efforts to ensure fairness, equality, and transparency for all partners, based on relative contribution and need.
- Several recent programs, including the C-17 GISP program in particular, provide insights into several specific policy measures that, based on program experience, facilitate a more successful program structure for spares pooling involving the USAF. These policy measures include the following issues and factors:

- U.S. export control laws and regulations can be a significant barrier to successful spares pooling. The most successful past programs have mitigated this problem by retaining U.S. ownership of all spares except when they are installed in allied-owned aircraft. In the case of C-17, Boeing, as the single point exporter, controls and allocates parts until they are installed on allied aircraft.
- Two critical keys to the success of configuration control and encouragement of innovation on the C-17 GISP program include (1) the requirement that all aircraft in the pool conform to U.S. configuration standards, with the proviso that (2) the USAF pays for the nonrecurring costs of upgrading the aircraft.
- Contract incentives for the prime contractor to meet international fleetwide performance metrics and priorities require a splitting out of the smaller foreign fleets with separately calculated metrics so that these fleets are serviced with the same priority as the larger U.S. fleet.
- The above factors may only work well in a program in which the U.S. fleet is significantly larger than all foreign fleets and in which the USAF is clearly the dominant customer, as in the case of the C-17 GISP program. This situation may not hold equally well for the F-35 program, particularly for such variants as the F-35B, for which U.S. dominance may not be nearly as clear-cut.

References

916 Starfighter, "Lockheed F-104 Starfighter," July 3, 2014. As of April 15, 2015:
http://www.916-starfighter.de/number_productionstatistic.htm

Beer, Francis A., *Integration and Disintegration in NATO: Processes for Alliance Cohesion and Prospects for the Atlantic Community*, Columbus, Ohio: Ohio State University Press, 1969.

British Broadcasting Corporation, BBC News, "RAF Typhoon Jets Grounded Owing to Spares Shortages," April 15, 2011.

Comptroller and Auditor General, United Kingdom National Audit Office, *Ministry of Defence: Management of the Typhoon Project,* HC 755 Session 2010–2011, London, HMSO, March 2, 2011.

Congress of the United States, The Congressional Budget Office, *NATO Burden Sharing After Enlargement*, Washington, D.C., August 2001.

Cornell, Alexander H., *International Collaboration in Weapons and Equipment Development and Production by the NATO Allies: Ten Years Later and Beyond*, Boston, Mass.: Kluwar, 1981.

Defence News Defence Talk Forum, "Will Latest F-35 Problems Push Norway Towards a European Solution?" September 19, 2008. As of April 15, 2015:
http://www.defencetalk.com/forums/

Defense Industry Daily, "NH90: Europe's Medium Helicopter Contender," August 5, 2013. As of April 15, 2015:
https://www.defenseindustrydaily.com/
nh90-europes-medium-helicopter-contender-04135/#2002andEarlier

Defense Industry Daily staff, "The Global C-17 Sustainment Partnership," *Defense Industry Daily*, January 17, 2013. As of April 15, 2015:
http://www.defenseindustrydaily.com/
did-focus-the-c17-global-sustainment-partnership-02756/

Drury, Ian, "RAF Strips Jets for Spare Parts: Typhoons Torn Up for Libya Air Fleet," *Daily Mail,* June 16, 2011.

European Defense Agency, European Union, *Study on the Innovative and Competitive Potential of the Defense Supplier Base in the EU12*, Brussels, 2009.

European Defense Agency, European Union, *EDA's Pooling and Sharing*, Brussels, November 24, 2011.

"Eurofighter Receives Typhoon Support Contract From NETMA," *Airforce Technology*, April 2, 2012.

Ferraro, Stacy N., "The European Defence Agency: Facilitating Defense Reform or Forming Fortress Europe?" *Transnational Law & Contemporary Problems*, No. 16-2, January 2007.

Giannangeli, Marco, "RAF Hit by Crisis Over Spares for Fighter Jets: Nearly Half the RAF's New Typhoon Jets Are Grounded Because of Maintenance and Lack of Spare Parts," *The Daily Express*, December 4, 2011.

Gunston, Bill, "MRCA," in *Attack Aircraft of the West*, Charles Scribner's Sons, New York, 1974.

Hastings, David, "Squadron Service, Target Lock: Eurofighter Typhoon," last updated December 28, 2012. As of August 9, 2013:
http://www.targetlock.org.uk/typhoon/service.html

House of Commons, Public Accounts Committee, Written Evidence, *Typhoon Public Accounts Committee Hearing, Supplementary Evidence*, April 4, 2010. As of April 15, 2015:
http://www.publications.parliament.uk/pa/cm201011/cmselect/cmpubacc/860/860we01.htm

IFS, IFS Applications Global Marketing Brochure, *Eurofighter GmbH Case Study*, September 2006.

Jennings, Gareth, "UK MoD Saves Money on Tornado and Harrier Programs," *Jane's Defence Weekly*, July 19, 2007.

Knaack, Marcelle Size, *Encyclopedia of US Air Force Aircraft and Missile Systems, Vol. 1, Post-World War II Fighters, 1945–1973*, Office of Air Force History, Washington, D.C., 1978.

Mechtersheimer, Alfred, *MRCA Tornado. Rüstung und Politik in der Bundesrepublik*, Osang Verlag, 1982.

McGarvey, Ronald G., Edward G. Keating, John G. Drew, Mark A. Lorell, James Pita, Daniel M. Romano, Joseph V. Vesely, and Robert A. Guffey, *Risks from U.S. Air Force Participation in the F-35 Global Spares Pool and Prospective Mitigations to Those Risks*, unpublished RAND Corporation research, 2013.

McGarvey, Ronald G., Edward G. Keating, Mark A. Lorell, James Pita, John G. Drew, Daniel M. Romano, Joseph V. Vesely, and Robert A. Guffey, *United States Air Force Participation in the F-35 Global Spares Pool: Advantages and Risks*, unpublished RAND Corporation research, 2015.

North Atlantic Treaty Organization, *NATO AEW&C Programme Management Organisation*, September 2012.

North Atlantic Treaty Organization, Joint Air Power Competence Centre, *Regional Fighter Partnership: Options for Cooperation and Cost Sharing*, Kalkar, Germany, March 2012.

North Atlantic Treaty Organization Helicopter Management Agency, *Common Spares Management: A Possible Way Forward, ISS WG 3*, briefing, March 13, 2013a.

North Atlantic Treaty Organization Helicopter Management Agency, *Materiel Support ISS WG 3 Topic 2.3*, briefing, Aix-en-Provence, March 13, 2013b.

North Atlantic Treaty Organization Maintenance and Supply Organization/Agency, *Delivering Effective Logistics Support, 50th Anniversary*, Luxembourg, 2008.

Osborne, Tony, "NH90 Faces Up to European Budget Cuts," *Aviation Week and Space Technology*, June 17, 2013.

Penney, Stewart, "Eurofighter Deal Nears Signature," *Flight International*, July 2, 2001.

Smith, Major General Homer D. (Ret), "NATO Maintenance and Supply Agency," *Army Logistician*, November–December 1986.

Tigner, Brooks, "EDA Must Step Up Capability Pooling Efforts, Says Senior Official," *Jane's Defence Industry,* February 4, 2011.

Tigner, Brooks, "Addressing the 'S' Word," *Jane's Defence Weekly*, February 25, 2013.

"Tornado Maintenance Contracts Pave Way for 'Future Contracting for Availability,'" *Defense Industry Daily*, December 20, 2005.

United Kingdom House of Commons, Committee of Public Accounts, Management of the Typhoon Project, Thirteenth Report of Session 2010–2012, London, HMSO, April 15, 2011.

United Kingdom National Audit Office, Comptroller and Auditor General, *Transforming Logistics Support for Fast Jets*, House of Commons 825 Sessions 2006–2007, July 17, 2007.

United Kingdom National Audit Office, Comptroller and Auditor General, *Ministry of Defence: Management of the Typhoon Project,* House of Commons 755 Session 2010–2011, London, HMSO, March 2, 2011.

"Vital Support Service," *Vortex Magazine: News from Eurofighter*, United Kingdom, Issue 3, 2001.

Western European Union, *Memoranda of Understanding WEU Mutual Emergency Logistics Support (MELS)*, CM (99)-52, November 1999.